My Modena

Praise for My Modena

Join Andrea Gelfuso and her family as they spend an enchanted year in Italy! You will laugh along with her as she navigates cultural differences and be charmed by her descriptions of the ancient, cobblestoned streets and alleyways. As she so aptly sums up her experience: "(Her) Modena is a painting, with a million strokes, of shade and light and subtle color. It's a thousand years of history . . . there is a language of bells." I loved this book!

~Susan Pohlman, author of *Halfway to Each Other: How a Year in Italy Brought our Family Home* and *A Time to Seek: Meaning, Purpose, and Spirituality at Midlife*

My Modena is a scrumptious literary tiramisu, layered with history, art, food, fashion, culture (and culture shock), all topped with generous dollops of hilarity.

On a year-long stint in Italy, Andrea Gelfuso proves the best of companions—self-deprecating, searingly honest and irrepressibly amused and amusing. She captures the trials and terrors that few travel guides mention, from card-eating ATMs, intimidating cashiers, aloof clerks and indecipherable instructions to impeccably styled women and drop-dead-gorgeous men.

In crisis after crisis, when all else fails, humor saves the day. We laugh with Andrea as she negotiates the maze of Italian streets, the humiliation of buying jeans (and a bathing suit!), the impenetrable mysteries of Italian washing machines, the despair of an Italian post office. It is pure pleasure to share Andrea's adventures and to experience Italy in all its colors and flavors through her unblinking eyes and with her magnanimous spirit.

Brava, Andrea, for bringing your Modena to life!

~Dianne Hales, New York Times bestselling author of *La Bella Lingua*, *Mona Lisa* and *La Passione*

My Modena is an utterly hilarious memoir of expat life in Modena, Italy. In Kafka-meets-David-Sedaris prose, Andrea Gelfuso recounts her epic battles to buy stamps, get mail, and recharge her phone. The laughs accentuate a tender love story as she falls for her adopted city, with its long history, exquisite food, and brutally chic denizens. A delight!

~Christina Lynch, New York Times bestselling author of *The Italian Party*

Andrea Gelfuso captures humorist Erma Bombeck's spirit of self-deprecation through a romp of a memoir that offers a window into her own soul.

~Teri Rizvi, founder and director, *Erma Bombeck Writers' Workshop*

Let's follow Andrea, the heroine of this book, in her adventures in Modena, Italy, fighting against red tape, the metric system, post offices closed all the time, perfidious ATMs sucking her debit cards and another thousand ordeals.

Notice the title: MY Modena. Her love for Modena is unshaken by any obstacles.

When Mark Twain arrived in Italy, at Bellagio on the Lago di Como, he was "fumigated", that is to say smoked as if he were a salmon, because there was an epidemic of cholera. He never forgot that experience and I think he never forgave Italians. If Andrea had been in Mark Twain's shoes, she would have hardly noticed it, because she looks at life through rose-tinted glasses and finds the funny side of it.

~Pier Antonio Pelloni

My Modena

A Year of Fear, Laughter, and Exhilaration in Italy

Andrea Susan Valentine Gelfuso Goetz

Storytellers Publishing
An *Imprint* of Journey Institute Press

Storytellers Publishing
An imprint of Journey Institute Press,
a division of 50 in 52 Journey, Inc.

journeyinstitutepress.com
Commerce City, CO USA 80022

Library of Congress Catalog Card Number pending
Names: Goetz, Andrea Susan Valentine Gelfuso
Title: My Modena: A Year of Fear, Laughter, and Exhilaration in Italy
Description: Colorado : Storytellers Publishing, 2021
Identifiers: ISBN 9781737359104 (softcover) |
ISBN 9781737359128 (hardcover) | ISBN 9781737359111 (e-book) |
ISBN 9781737359135 (audio book)
Subjects: BISAC: TRAVEL / Europe / Italy |
TRAVEL / Special Interests / Family | TRAVEL / General.

First Edition

Printed in the United States of America
10 9 8 7 6 5 4 3 2 1

Set in Garamond

I'm deeply grateful to all of the people who made this book possible, especially:

My husband, Andy, who gave me the world, handled logistics, and believes in train maps – and me. I'll love you forever.

My kids Alex and Annalise, who made every step of our travels an adventure, including our pathetic "Little Train" trip to Sassuolo. I wish you two every joy of a life lived with purpose, living your dreams, and most of all, love.

To my publishers Michael and Dafna, who made this book happen. I can't thank you enough for taking this journey with me.

My Grandma Jane, who taught me the magic of stories.

My Grandfather Harry, who introduced me to humor writers who have been my comfort and delight since childhood.

Maria, who helped me see the beauty of Italy before I knew how to pronounce "Modena."

To Mary-Ann, the best yoga teacher ever, who gave me the story that led me to my publishers, and gave me, literally, strength.

To my Yoga Buddies, who created a community to keep us connected through Covid.

To the talented and supportive members of the Journey Institute Press Writers Alumni Group, who encouraged me when I was one comma from giving up.

To all of my family and friends who made me laugh and feel loved, including Paula, the best sister in the world, and to Olga, Barbara, and Jen, who walked with me and kept me reasonably sane, and Eileen, who has the heart of a poet and the soul of a warrior.

To Bunny, who carried boxes of our books when we moved – I hope you like this one.

To Lauren, my Accountability Buddy. You inspire me. ONWARD!

To Carolyn, the best human in the world.

To the City of Modena, and all of her gorgeous sons and daughters.

And to all of you reading this, if you want to write a book, and you know you do, find a group of supportive friends and writers. Whining is fine, just keep going.

-AG

Preface

My husband and kids and I spent a year in Modena, Italy, where people wearing fabulous shoes make Maseratis, Ferraris, and *aceto balsamico* (sweet vinegar). And Modena made me deliriously happy. As I wandered the meandering streets, the ancient ochre buildings draped around my shoulders like a richly woven scarf. Surrounded by chattering crowds in Piazza Grande, Italian vowels rolled over me like a mahogany river, and I felt a vibration deep in my chest: I was purring.

My loveliest memory from that year is the sound of our four rolling suitcases rumbling over cobblestones to catch a train to another adventure: in 2009 we traveled to over 50 European cities. I carried a tiny notebook to jot down notes for over 60 funny stories I wrote for my friends. We laughed about my painfully stunning Italian neighbor, ("Fabio On the Balcony") about gorgeous Italian firefighters in their bucket truck letting my family back into our 7th floor apartment, ("Rescue Me") and about surviving a bike ride against a geriatric opponent on my 50-year-old bike ("Bella").

My stories were mostly about my fear and embarrassment at my inability to complete the most basic of tasks. Most essential government services were *chiuso*, (closed) most of the time, and when offices were open, they were focused on preventing progress—Italian postal clerks Would. Not. Sell. Me. A. Stamp. Buying a cellphone and keeping it stocked with voices required 800 forms of identification and a DNA sample, and it took three months and an epic battle with my US bank, the US Post Office, and FedEx to replace a debit card that was confiscated by an ATM when I was trying to buy groceries.

The whole time I was in Italy I was afraid—to buy a phone ("Phonezilla"); to buy a stamp ("Deliver This"); to find the street market ("All Was Not Lost, But I Was"); and to buy clothes ("Agoraphobia Means I Miss TJ Maxx") until the magical moment I bought a fabulous Italian gown ("Piccolina").

But these stories are also about learning to push past boundaries I built based on my fear. My fear of getting lost in Byzantine streets. My fear of the Italian language and learning the difference between *spingere*, (to push) and *tirare*, (to pull). My inability to remember the meaning of those words when approaching a door created another fear—of being embarrassed. And yet what wonders lay beyond those doors—Renaissance art, Italian fashion, laughter in unfamiliar syllables. Learning to let go of my fears opened Italy to me.

Tirare—pull; *spingere*—push. These signs hung on most entryways, and I always chose wrong. I couldn't learn the difference, and it made me hesitate to open doors, to avoid looking like a fool. But living well—in any country—is about learning to enjoy what you don't know, and opening every door, anyway.

Part I

Introduction

How many books written by men open with the writer sobbing on the floor?

Weirdly, many women's memoirs do. Women's adventures start with tears because women automatically apologize for doing something awesome.

Not me, Bub.

My Italian adventure began with laughter and profanity. When my husband, Andy, a geography professor, wanted to discuss his upcoming sabbatical, I beamed. Sitting at our kitchen table, he asked two of my favorite questions:

"Where do you want to go?"

I laughed. "Italy!"

"How long do you want to stay?"

"F**k' it—a year!"

At the time I didn't know that we'd be gone for the year of the Great Recession and an international banking crisis that would target my personal debit card, or that I'd come back to a job market that would make it hard to recover lost ground. But spending a year in Italy with my husband and two kids—living in a town that had celebrated beauty for centuries, and climbing onto trains and low-cost airlines to visit more than 50 European cities in 12 months—was worth it.

Breaking free of my toxic boss was one of my life's epic moments:

The staff meeting of 20 government lawyers and administrative staff presided over by a short, pudgy political hack was grinding to a close. "Does anyone have anything else?" Biff asked as he started to gather up his notes.

"I do. This is my last staff meeting. I'm going to Italy for a year."

"What?" he sputtered. His flaccid face flopped further.

"I'm leaving. I'm going to live in Italy. In Modena."

Modena is in Northern Italy and is the home of Maserati, Ferrari, and balsamic vinegar. I know Biff knew where Modena was; he spent college summers playing tennis there.

"You're going to live in Modena?" Biff's pale face puffed up like a marshmallow in a microwave. Half of my co-workers had known this news for months and were trying not to laugh. It was a struggle to keep from replying, "Oh, so that means you *weren't* bugging my office?"

That staff meeting was the first one in months that I hadn't dreaded. I didn't hate my job; I hated my bullying boss. When I had to meet with him for my performance evaluation, a co-worker advised me to think of something I *liked* about him. I took a walk and realized: "If Biff wasn't so awful, I wouldn't be taking this incredible step." I went into the meeting with a huge smile on my face.

A year in Italy was one of my many leaps off the adventure cliff. In college I worked on an island off the East Coast at Mario's, an Italian restaurant where mobsters gathered for weekly confabs. On Sunday mornings Paulie, the head chef, closed the restaurant and a clump of extras from *The Godfather* movies shuffled in. Doze guys wore trench coats over thick square suits with somber shirts, disconcertingly pastel ties, and black fedoras. On a resort island. In August. "Bring us cawfee an' stay outta the dining room!" barked Paulie, a man as small, gray, and prickly as a used Brillo pad.

While I worked during the day for an island housecleaning service, at the restaurant my official job title was "salud gull." Six nights a week I sloshed oily dressing on heaps of iceberg lettuce and prepped cold dishes like antipasto and raw oysters. Steam rose from the grill as Paulie bellowed orders to Ryan, the Cali surfer-dude sous chef. "Linguini reehhddd!! Linguini whhhyyyydte!"

Mario's was uneasily perched like a restless seagull next to a tiny harbor. With the windows left open to ocean breezes, flies flecked the kitchen until Paulie sprayed a clotted stream of insecticide over every sticky surface and open container of food—the grill sizzling with meat, the steam table soaking soggy vegetables, the greasy cutting boards and counters, and the wide-mouthed buckets of salad dressing.

One Cessna-sized fly escaped the onslaught but ran out of gas on a plate of antipasto. A reedy waiter returned from the dining room with the massive corpse grotesquely weighing down a lettuce leaf and shrieked, "The customer is disgusted!! There was a fly in his salad!! I need a new one!!"

Paulie plunged his filthy hands into the lettuce, yanked out the fly, re-fluffed the salad, and shoved it back at the waiter. "It's FIIINNNE!!" Terrified, the waiter returned to the dining room with his ankles wobbling like a toddler on an ice rink.

I once asked Paulie how to make cappuccino. Forty years later, I still marvel at how he grabbed a Bialetti espresso maker, filled the bottom with water, filled the funnel with coffee, screwed it shut, and slammed it onto the grill in one continuous and impossible-to-follow motion. I was too terrified to ask him again and didn't learn to make espresso until I was 57, from a YouTube video.

I tried not to talk to Paulie at all, but he asked me once where a pan was stored. I pointed and said, "Under there."

"Under where?" he growled.

And I replied, *to a Mob chef*, "You said underwear!!" His expression was a steel-plated door slamming shut; he didn't laugh, but he didn't kill me, either.

I left when a dispute over bonus pay led to an argument that Paulie resolved by locking his jaws onto the neck of Ryan the sous chef as the two of them rolled down the steep steps of an island hotel. Ryan, with the calm determination of a reasonable person, returned with his ER bill, saying, "You have to pay for this. Human bites are very dangerous; I needed stitches and a tetanus shot!

Paulie bellowed, "I'll getta coupla guys from da Hill to break your legs with a baseball bat. *Then* you'll know what's dangerous."

But he said underwear.

[Forty years later I still think this is hilarious.]

I put my salud gull experience to work in my next summer job, in a tourist restaurant in Yosemite National Park, where, as a "cold prep supervisor," I festively threaded orange slices with parsley and doled out cold salads to the waiters. The guy who made the salads was aptly named "Caesar," but inexplicably he would share only a few of his masterpieces at a time. When I needed to restock, I had to walk miles over greasy terracotta tiles, past the industrial dishwasher belching steam that was operated by a guy rhythmically bellowing, "I love the Curry Company!!! [*Smashes dinner plate.*] I love my job! [*Smash!*]"

Living in a national park where I sunbathed steps off the trail beside my own private waterfalls, I met Tom, a quiet Midwesterner who loved books, obsessed about the perfect backpacking packing list, and played a haunting "Dust in the Wind" on acoustic guitar. Over hikes to Yosemite

Falls and bottles of Martinelli's apple cider, we became a thing. Over lunch in the employee cafeteria, he mentioned that his friends were driving to Alaska to work in the salmon canneries and asked if I wanted to go. As peas rolled off my fork, I smiled. "Why the hell not?!"

I love that about me.

Like Cheryl Strayed in *Wild*, I was under-equipped for the rigors of the trail. I had a faded orange frame backpack, a high-strung guitar in a cheap cardboard case, and... who packs white farmer jeans to hitchhike to Alaska? Days later we celebrated Fourth of July by throwing our packs into an orange VW minibus with floral carpeted walls and a lovely lab named Sadie, who collected fist-sized rocks at every stop.

The van's owner was a scrawny pale slimeball with ratty Rasta braids who chatted amiably while squatting in the dirt to defecate. His girlfriend was lost in billowy cotton, but that's because they ate only bean sprout sandwiches, and he allotted her only a few sprouts per sandwich. To save money on ferry fares, he demanded that "the girls" hide under the VW's seats with Sadie's rocks. Not my travel style, and *definitely* not in white farmer jeans. Tom and I left them in a ferry parking lot lit by lodgepole pine streetlights. Topped by bald eagles, the light poles looked like macho swizzler sticks. Hissing yellow bulbs ominously drained color from the night, turning our terse goodbye into film noir.

Without a ride, we hitchhiked the rest of the way to Homer, Alaska, to spend a summer working in a salmon cannery. We lived in a backpacking tent on Homer Spit, on the beach behind the Shrimp Shack takeout joint. Fueled by peanut butter and canned kippers (a backpacking tent doesn't offer gourmet cooking options), we worked at least 12 hours a day, 7 days a week.

I spent those hours wedged in a corner, perched high above the cannery floor on an icy metal platform. Fishing boats brought salmon fresh from Alaskan waters packed in ice in huge metal bins. I operated a gear shift that controlled the rate at which the salmon fell from the bins onto the conveyor belt that carried them into the cannery to be sorted, gutted, and packaged for sale. Emptying the bins resulted in a continuous crescendo of blood, ice, and fish scales that splashed onto my hair and clothes like a "Pirates of the Caribbean" ride from hell.

The fish gutters had the toughest jobs. Fueled by overtime pay, caffeine, and assorted drugs, they worked more than 20-hour days. Lulled to sleep by exhaustion, the gutters' clothes—and sometimes a stray body part—snagged in the cannery machinery until they were cut out of the gears.

I can't look at a box of Sleepy Time tea — our evening break snack—without flashing back to an industrial break room lit by florescent lights bouncing off blood-slimed yellow fishing slickers and pants.

But that memory is softened by an evening in The Salty Dog, a bar for locals with a floor strewn with sawdust that was swept out at closing — 8 a.m. — and where a guitarist sang "Rocky Raccoon." While breathing in pine shavings among the wooled and weathered crowd, I expected Rocky to burst open the saloon doors and slam down a whiskey. In the darkness of the bar, I was grateful I had lived one of my favorite songs.

After several months, we were tired of being human chum. So we quit our jobs and hitchhiked to Denali, where we locked our salmon-scented clothes in bear lockers to protect us from grizzlies. At night, we lay on our backs watching the Aurora Borealis wave like an emerald silk scarf behind the Big Dipper. When a shooting star fell through the Swarovski crystals of the Dipper's handle, I knew all that mucking around in fish guts had been worth it.

So, when Andy asked if I wanted to spend a year living in Italy, I was in.

Chapter 1
We arrive!

We left Denver on a New Year's Eve red eye. "We" consisted of my husband, Andy, a college professor from Cleveland who had survived 16 years of marriage to me, and our kids, Alex, then 12, and Annalise, then 6.

We landed in Bologna in meteorological and mental fog, and boarded a bus that dropped us off directly across from our apartment in Modena. Our friend Melanie met us at the bus and dragged us to an ATM through winding streets and confusing odors while she rattled off instructions about how to deal with banks, telephones, and other essential services. I didn't understand anything she said, but over the next few months I learned that in Italy, "essential services" are neither, so it didn't matter.

Melanie, a high-end fashion consultant[1] who dresses impeccably for every occasion, had worked as a managing editor for the Italian version of GQ Magazine, and as Princess Stephanie of Monaco's private assistant. Although she is American, Melanie is an Italy-whisperer: when my bank card was sucked into a supermarket ATM in Modena, from her office in Milan, she directed a bank employee to open the machine and give me back my card.

The evening we arrived, our landlady, Giovanna, and her husband, Raimondo, graciously threw us a welcome dinner, with multiple tantalizing courses. Giovanna, a retired teacher, was welcoming and warm and suffused with light. She reminded me of saffron, the golden spice essential for real risotto. Raimondo, a retired art historian, was slight and soft spoken, with a quiet dignity. Their friends Piero and Annamaria were fascinating. Piero was an artist with an encyclopedic knowledge of Modena history, and Annamaria's pumpkin ravioli was an art form in itself. Also at dinner were Giovanna and Raimondo's daughter, Matilde, her husband, Marcello, and their daughter, whose gentle smiles were a comfort after a long and confusing day.

---

1   See www.Melaniepayge.com, or check out Melanie's fashion videos on YouTube. _

Suffering from jet lag, exhaustion, and trying to be social in an unfamiliar language, Andy and I struggled to converse using limited language skills and brains wrapped in soggy cotton batting. Our daughter Annalise, six and very shy, deployed her Little Kid Force Field and was exempt from communication. Our son Alex alternated between asking for more food and gently snoozing. He'd accept offers of cheese, smoked salmon, grilled vegetables, and pasta, but by the time the new item reached his plate, he'd have fallen back asleep until Giovanna's next offer jogged him awake.

Our year in Italy began with lovely Italians, incredible food, laughter, and confusion, and it pretty much stayed that way the whole time.

The commute from dinner to our apartment was mercifully short—just across the landing from Giovanna's. Fortunately, Giovanna didn't know then that Alex would create a mysterious stink in our apartment by forgetting sushi under his bed for six months, that Annalise would fill her room with plastic bottles and boxes for her "Creative Center," and that firefighters would have to use their bucket truck to enter our 7th-floor apartment when we couldn't open our three-inch-thick wooden door. And we didn't know then that living without a car meant we'd learn to love long walks, that living in another language meant we'd learn how it feels to be an outsider, and that being constantly confused is the hilarious essence of learning.

Chapter 2
Beginnings

After four days in Italy, the jet lag wore off and confusion set in. We'd spend all morning in various government offices attempting to comply with Italian immigration requirements, only to realize that neither we nor the Italian government had what was needed to accomplish what they wanted us to do. Dealing with Italian bureaucracy was a lot like playing *Myst*, with sound.

After futile office visits, we staggered to the grocery store to replenish our food supply. The market held many mysteries—what was the Italian word for bleach? What does *Pane morbido* mean? (It means "soft bread," which is a lot less dramatic in English than it looks in Italian.)

We had unlimited opportunities to discover the wonders of the grocery store because Alex was then 12 years old, and his appetite rivaled that of zoo tigers. Twenty minutes after a huge dinner, he was famished. Andy and I watched mutely as he finished off most of what was left in the minuscule refrigerator and then headed for the almost-empty pantry.

We had no car, and the nearest grocery store was a quarter mile away. Every walk to the store burned 100 calories. On the return trip, loaded down with bottles,[2] cans, and produce, we burned another 300. Annalise was only six years old, I was recovering from a broken wrist, and the four of us could carry maybe 10,000 calories per shopping run, but Alex consumed 2,000 calories per hour around the clock, the whole time we were in Italy, and the rest of us were ravenous from all the walking and the amazing Italian food. That first week we walked to the market almost every day. Although math wasn't my specialty, there was one thing I could count on: our family couldn't carry enough food to keep up with our rate of consumption, and we were going to starve to death.

---

2   After the second round of shopping, I did a cost/benefit ratio on each item our grocery list based on weight vs. nutritional value. When a kid asked for a bottle of juice, I said, "Only if you carry it home." Survival of the fittest is actually a thing.

While faint from hunger and awaiting my demise, I washed clothes. The ancient washer was a front loader with a mysterious assortment of dials and buttons from which the writing had long worn off. The clothes were trapped in the machine for at least two hours, maybe three. Sometimes the washer randomly decided it wouldn't release its door unless I allowed it another cycle; since I had no idea what any of the buttons were for, I was in no position to argue. I tried to wash a load of cleaning rags, but two hours and 16 minutes of laundering merely redistributed the dirt more equitably. By the time the washer was done with a load of the kids' clothes, they had outgrown them.

Chapter 3
Epiphany

Stava nevicando. It was snowing. An American with a minivan takes little notice of temperature and precipitation. But in Italy, where I had no car, no sense of direction, or even warm shoes, I was three snowflakes south of hypothermia and three degrees north of neurosis.

Fortunately, we were trapped like rats in our apartment. It was January 6th in Italy, *Epifania*, and everything was closed.

Chiuso.

In Italy, everything is closed most of the time. Italy is closed many mornings, all through lunch (1:00–3:30), most afternoons, all day Sunday, any day within three weeks of a holiday, and any time you want to buy a cellphone. Modena is also closed on Thursday afternoons, because hello, who needs a cellphone?

Chiuso.

It's not that there was a huge incentive to go outside. Modena in winter is damp and cold. January's weather forecast featured festive bouts of icy fog laced with foggy ice. Giovanna kindly drove us to several government offices. Scoffing at my cloth coat, she offered a fur one. And a fur hat.

Missy Environmentalist recoiled in horror. I do not wear the pelts of dead animals. But then we stepped outside. When the jagged blade of silvered frost slashed at my throat and hands, I *understood* fur. I wanted to hunt down something large and hairy, kill it myself, and wrap its still-warm body around my pathetic wool coat.[3]

Now *there's* an epiphany.

---

3   Actually, the hat and coat were fake fur. Phew.

Chapter 4
We Can't Comfortably Sit Down for an Entire Year

Our apartment was on the 7th floor of an obstinately thick building. We had a balcony that overlooked a cantaloupe-colored train station, with tiny tin trains that passed soundlessly beyond the trees. The cars were charming commuter coaches with varnished wooden walls and seats; as we clacked along, I had a hard time not shrieking, "Isn't this ADORABLE??!"

We signed our apartment lease in a crypt-like conference room nestled into the walls of one of Modena's oldest buildings. To reach the office, we strolled along a lovely curving arcade until our landlord, Raimondo, stopped and pushed a button on the wall. Silently, a pair of medieval wooden doors swung open. They were curved at the top, thick enough to withstand a siege, and tall enough to admit a man on horseback. As the doors opened, I expected to find a knight politely waiting to exit.

We entered an inner courtyard shaded in stone and lined with columns, and were ushered into a conference room. The lease signing ceremony was fascinating because it involved so many people: Andy and me, Raimondo, Eugenia, a representative from the tenant's union who represented our interests, a translator, and someone from the City. Raimondo was also entitled to have a representative from the landlords' union, but he declined. *This* is why Italian offices are always closed—everyone is at a lease signing ceremony.

The translator and our union rep were late. While we waited, we tried to speak with Raimondo, but all of his brilliant knowledge of Italian history and art was lost to me until I could learn more Italian. We helpfully conjugated the verb *lavorare*, "to work," and then Andy wanted to show off his understanding of the past tense. "I took the train yesterday," he said in Italian. Raimondo looked unimpressed. "I'm not just saying that, I really did it!!" I wanted to pat Andy on the head and say, "Good BOOOY!" but the humor was lost on both of them.

The apartment itself, with erratic electricity and primordial plumbing, was like camping, with tile.[4] Although the building was post-war, the amenities were Bronze Age. Electricity was anything but current. If we used more than one volt of electricity, we were plunged into darkness, and Raimondo would patiently flip the circuit breaker with a sigh. *Again?*

The entire kitchen could fit into a refrigerator box. There was an elfin stove, and a sink that spat water that was occasionally warm, but was usually icy or lethally hot, and often sulfurous. Because the tap water tasted like rusty bolts and could probably be used to patch metal, we hauled our drinking water, in six packs of two-liter plastic bottles, from a shop several blocks away. Without a car, even drinking water, we burned calories.

The refrigerator was the size of a Barbie Dream Van, but with Alex eating three times his weight at every meal, we never had leftovers, so it didn't matter. The counter was a narrow ledge where I chopped mountains of vegetables. As I chopped, I listened to Pavarotti sing in the melancholy colors of Modena—the ochre and burnt melon and citrine of the stucco walls and clay tile I could see through the small kitchen window.

---

4   Our rent money was used to renovate the apartment for our landlords' fabulous daughter. When we visited years after leaving Modena, the kitchen cabinets were chic mahogany, and there was a…dishwasher?!

The kitchen drawers were stocked with mystifying cooking implements and/or possibly diabolical torture devices, and the cabinets glittered with glassware and dishes in every size, from thimble to flower petal. Besides smoking incessantly and having to carry 40-lb packs of water, Italians may stay so thin because their plates are so small. Sadly, in the course of a year, I shattered most of those glasses on the ceramic tile floor. In a Modena museum, Annalise and I marveled at ancient Etruscan glassware that had survived eons of earthquakes, wars, and drunken relatives. Annalise wisely observed: "Mom, it's a good thing you never worked as a curator."

Like the plates, the apartment's furniture was Lilliputian, including a couch big enough for all of us to sit on if none of us had eaten recently, and a coffee table that, because it was glass, I also broke. The dining area had French doors that were actually Italian and led onto a narrow balcony. There was a long wooden table with hard wooden chairs, and a blonde banquet that fortuitously held extra glassware. Beside the door was a fully loaded umbrella stand, which should have tipped us off to Modena's actual climate. Sunny Italy? Good luck with that!

The master bedroom held a bed, two teeny chairs, an armoire, and a dresser, all from Louie the XIV's doll house. Each miniature door and drawer had its own key, which made me think Italians didn't have a lot of stuff, but they had a lot to hide.

Alex had the largest room with a massive armoire and a sleigh bed. Looming over his bed was a huge painting of two ice-blue, smooth-limbed, and faceless lovers who cowered beneath a smooth blue Jesus who sagged ominously from an enormous cross. I'm not sure what drifting off and waking up under an acrylic depiction of "The Blue Man Group Meets Crucified Jesus" did to Alex's dreams or mental health, but it never affected his appetite, so there's that.

Annalise's room had a painted armoire, an iron bedstead so tall she could play under it and dramatically fall out of it, and a cabinet into which she stuffed plastic water bottles and empty (we hoped) food cartons into a "Creativity Center" that was more like an all-inclusive resort for vermin.

The apartment had two bathrooms, if you counted a mop closet that contained a toilet. The main bathroom was light and airy, but had a toilet inexplicably designed with a sandpapery rear wall. There were two flushing options: a quick rinse for *numero uno*, and a more forceful blast for *numero due,* but the poop-catcher wall held onto the goods no matter how many times you flushed; a fair warning for subsequent visitors was: "I pushed the big button!"

The shower was under no pressure to release water; in the morning, I could cry harder than the trickle that sullenly emerged from the shower head.

And soon you will learn why that bathroom left me flushed for more than the usual reasons.

Chapter 5
Alone Again, Unnaturally

Most days Andy took the adorable train to his office in Bologna, and the kids rode a mauve bus to school. Because Andy and the kids were gone all day, and I was afraid to leave, I spent a lot of time alone in the apartment. That wasn't great for my sanity, and I deteriorated a lot faster than I expected. Here's what I wrote after only two weeks:

It's raining again. Some people think gray skies are soothing. Those are crazy people, and they should all move to Seattle, where they're out of the way and can't hurt anyone. I don't do well without sunlight. I'm starting to feel like Boo Radley, the recluse from To Kill a Mockingbird *who didn't see the sun for 35 years. That can't be good, because there are scissors in the chifforobe.*

Oh Lordy, it seems like only yesterday I was a lawyer who identified with Atticus Finch. Two weeks of rain, and I'm getting more off kilter than the dog Atticus took out with a single shot.

It can't keep raining, or I'm going to demand a retraction on that "Sunny Italy" claim. After five soggy days of denial, I bought a cheap umbrella. But I'd be better off with one of those little paper umbrellas you get in tropical drinks; at least those open and close more than once. All of this friction between the water molecules is going to wear out the clouds, eventually. Or maybe the constant rubbing of water against cloud fluff will make the soft parts pill, like a cheap sweater. I think you can remove that with scissors; that will give me something to do until the rain stops. Or maybe I'll make a little boy, a little girl, out of wax.

Do you hear howling? Or is it me?

When it rains, I don't go to the grocery store, because I have no car, and I do not like to carry bags of produce while swimming. But that makes me a wimp. In Modena, biking to the store in the rain is just another way for Italian old people to show that they are tougher than American Hells Angels. In this city, the oldest citizens ride bicycles to the market, while holding umbrellas, in traffic. Drivers dodge and weave, moving so fast that they braid the air surrounding the bicyclists, who, enclosed within horizontal sheets of water, peddle serenely on. If America is ever invaded by Italian senior citizen bicyclists, it's all over.

If it's raining, I'm usually in the apartment. If I'm home, I'm washing clothes. I don't know how we end up with so many dirty clothes. I'm beginning to suspect that the children have multiple personalities, each with a separate wardrobe. This is a problem because the washer here holds only three socks at a time, two socks if they're dirty. It takes two hours to wash a load, and for every one of the 120 minutes the washer is running, it makes a disturbing noise.

Between cycles, the washer beeps maniacally, like a Fiat enraged by a cyclist. When the washer is spinning, which it does 40 times in two hours, it sounds like a jumbo jet is landing in the hallway. The washer is apparently afraid of planes—at the end of every spin cycle, it tries to escape by thrashing against every available surface, including the ceiling. To minimize the shaking, I can either sit on the washer for two hours, or heave the heaviest thing in the apartment, an old metal toolbox, onto the washer. But every third load, the washer manages to throw off the toolbox with a thunderous crash, which can't endear us to our downstairs neighbors. That may explain the popping sounds and the bullet casings in the hallway.

Fortunately, I bought Alex an electric guitar, so the shrieks coming from his amplifier will drown out the noise from our washer. A thoughtful response to legitimate concerns is the key to good neighbor relations.

Another fun rainy-day activity is sweeping. I sweep because the children are feral, and after every meal there are globs of food the size of cats under the table; the biggest chunks work well as ottomans. But even without the food debris, there is dust everywhere. It's not just a light dusting of dust, there's a living fiber beast that sheds grayish navy-blue clumps. The clumps collect hair, farm implements, and lawn furniture. No matter how many times I sweep, there's another wad to replace it, and if I swipe up a large bit, I hear growling. Somewhere in the apartment, a secret door leads to the lair of a molting Yeti, but unfortunately, it doesn't eat table scraps.

I could sweep for two hours straight between washer loads. When the washer finally lets go of the clothes, I hang them on racks in the apartment. Not even wealthy people in Italy have dryers, because dryers require industrial-grade wiring, and who needs that when you can get the same jolt from espresso?

While I hang out the clothes, I sing mournful songs about American laborers, like James Taylor's "Millworker," or Paul Simon's "American Tune." I warble dirges to make my children feel guilty about how hard I'm working. It's not having the desired effect.

One afternoon, taking a break from hanging out the clothes, I sat down in Alex's room. "Why are you just sitting around in my room?" he demanded. "I'm the one who just sits around in my room."

Our eyes met. "It's my life has been wasted, and I have been a fooool...."

After Alex finished hanging up the clothes, I made him sweep.

On sunny days, I go to the roof and hang things there. There is a clothesline on the roof, and the view from the roof is of a miniature Modena; the city looks like a Lionel train set from the 1940s. The little trains bump along, and the little cars in the roundabout try to kill each other, and pedestrians, in a charmingly tiny way.

To reach the roof I climb a steeply angled iron ladder. This is tricky with a large basket of clothes, a small box of clothespins, and a huge fear of spiders. At the very top of the ladder, there is a steel door that opens with a skeleton key. Skeleton keys got their name because all the people who used them ended up skeletons. The top of the ladder is totally dark except for the light through the keyhole. To open the door, I balance the basket against my hip, fumble with the key, and wait to be tapped on the shoulder by a large and hissing spider. The anticipation of the spider's tap makes me want to drop the basket.

Once, I dropped the key. Straight down, through the ladder, into a pile of junk that was stacked at the end of WWII and has since become a convention center for carnivorous spiders. The junk consisted of vertically stacked windows and shutters, so to find the key I had to reeeach in between them and feeeeel around in 60 years' worth of dirt and spider webs. I still have a twitch from that episode. If I ever drop the key again, I'll just wear all our wet clothes and drape myself over the balcony.

Every night I take out the garbage. When we first arrived, Giovanna took us to the grocery store. When, still in Costco mode, I kept searching the aisles for garbage bags, Giovanna looked at me like I was a lunatic. Hello, you don't need to buy garbage bags, you re-use the plastic ones you get from the grocery store. But since you're charged a few cents for every grocery bag, you have to buy bags one way or another. There are perfectly valid reasons to think that I am a lunatic (Andy would be helpful on this subject), so I didn't think my American reliance on garbage bags was all that odd. But in this country, if you can't ride a bike in the rain, you have no moral authority, so I still use the store grocery bags.

Grocery store bags are small and fill up quickly, so I empty the garbage every night; I take the garbage to the dumpster outside the building. I usually wait until after dinner when it's dark. We're on the 7th floor, and the hall staircase is lit by a light on a timer. I hit the hall light switch on the way down the stairs, but there's never enough time to get to the dumpster and back up seven flights of stairs before the light goes off.

We live off a busy traffic circle that spits Fiats onto our little street like bullets. Our building's trash dumpster was thoughtfully placed between the sidewalk and the busiest part of the traffic circle. One side of the dumpster is impossible to open, and the other side opens easily, with a bar that you press with your foot. Of course, the side of the dumpster with the foot bar is not the one facing the sidewalk; the foot bar is directly in the line of traffic speeding around the circle. So, to throw out the trash I walk into traffic, step on the foot bar, heave the garbage in, and attempt to return to our building alive. All of this takes a while, so the stairway light is close to turning off by the time I get back into the building.

There's no way to give yourself more time on the hall light—you have to wait for the light to go out before you can turn it on again. When the light goes out, the hallway is completely dark, and a person in mid-step stands an excellent chance of falling down the stairs, which would end badly, because the stairs are made of marble. Cheap marble, but cartwheeling down a flight of cheap marble hurts just as much as the expensive kind. I take the stairs two at a time and go as fast as I can. As I climb the stairs, I hold onto the banister in case the light goes out, and pause on each landing. The light usually goes off when I'm between floors four and five.

One night I was particularly spry at getting the garbage in the dumpster and I got back up the stairs in record time. I made it all the way to the 5th floor, and I knew the light would go out soon, so I just waited on the landing. There is a hall light button switch on each floor, next to the buzzer for each apartment door. I was winded, so just outside Apartment Number 8, I waited for the staircase light to go off. My hand was poised above the hall light switch, and I leaned against the wall, breathing like Boo after the knife fight with Mr. Ewing.

Although the hall was usually empty, just as the hall light clicked off, the door to Apartment Number 8 opened, and when a woman in her night gown walked onto the landing, I gasped. I was too surprised to move, and the woman must have been freaked that a crazy American was breathing heavily on her doorbell in the dark.

At least I wasn't holding a Costco garbage bag, that would be crazy.

Chapter 6
Baggage

Soon after we arrived, the sky seeped a slow, surly rain. Like a cat or any other sane species, I don't like getting my feet wet. I didn't bring a raincoat; I couldn't fit a raincoat in my luggage. When we packed for our year in Italy, the four of us could each take two suitcases weighing 50 euros each. Or 50 kilometers—I never get that right. But anyway, there were limits, so I brought two pairs of pajamas, two pairs of shoes, and four black turtlenecks. I didn't have *room* for a raincoat.

Andy, who was theoretically under the same luggage weight restriction, had a specialized outfit for every occasion, including Amish barn raisings and underwater weddings. His carry-on must have been the carpet bag that Mary Poppins used to furnish her room. He had a raincoat, sweaters in every texture and hue, heaps of t-shirts, and pants in every length and fabric. I suspected that for spring, he'd pull out fashion-forward Man Capris.

Why did he bring all those clothes? This man could pack for a week using only a Pez dispenser. And his clothes are huge, of a size not found in nature. He's 6'4" (that's 20 stone in the metric system) and an extremely long-limbed individual. My entire wardrobe weighed less than a pair of his socks. I am 5 feet tall and was a size 2-4, and I had to leave behind my pajamas with buttons because the extra thread was too heavy.

I did not understand how he got all those clothes to Italy, and when I changed from my pajamas into a black turtleneck, it irked me. I am extremely irkable, but being perpetually dressed for Marcel Marceau's funeral did not help.

The last straw came on a sloshy, slushy day, when I made a hideous discovery. You think you know someone, and then, like a pedestrian staying to the far right of the bike path, I was hit from out of nowhere. I looked over to find that Andy was wearing... winter boots. His winter boots were heavy, old leather—the dirt on them weighed more than I did.

I had a flashback to the final moments of packing for Italy: When I wondered whether to bring boots for the kids, Andy scoffed—*scoffed*, I tell you! In a scoffy voice he said, "We don't have that much room in the suitcases. They won't *need* boots." I didn't have room in my suitcase either, what with taking shirts covered in oxygen, so I left *my* boots at home. And so, on a chilling February day, when one of my two allotted winter shoes was soaking up dirty ice and snow and the slush was seeping into my ankles, I looked down and… Andy was wearing BOOOTS?!! These are the moments the insanity defense is made for.

Nothing generates literary inspiration like a stroll with your spouse. So, here's a poem Andy inspired, called "Let's Talk About the Relationship":

&&@@!!* **##!!!

@*&*&@#(@#&!!

@!!

Poetry, like packing and marriage, is all about baggage.

Although I was slowly going insane from the rain, being alone, and being with a spouse who brought rain gear and BOOOTS, in the good news, I was shocked by Italians for a delightfully crazy reason.

Chapter 7
Impossibly Gorgeous Italians

Like a movie with jump scares in reverse, Italy kept me on edge from unexpected encounters with heart-stoppingly gorgeous Italians. You can't swing a tortellini without hitting one, especially on a train.

When I visited my friend Melanie in Milan, my phone died in trainsit; I needed help to find a phone in the station to let Mel know when I'd arrive.

Milan's train station teems with travelers and is rife with pick pockets, so I was nervous about finding a phone while holding onto my socks, wallet, and original hair color. The only person sharing my train compartment was a lumpish man of indeterminate age who was grunting into a phone curled under his neck. As we pulled into the station, I tapped him gently, and asked if he could help me. Like a time-lapse video of a mud-sodden seed blossoming into a spectacular flower, Signore Treno sat up, lowered his sunglasses, and revealed the face and physique of a young, Italian, George Clooney. He said his name was Danilo, and when he smiled, I saw constellations.

Too late to back out of my request for assistance, I clawed together words in English and Italian and heaped them into workable phrases. He gently took my rolling carry on, and we chatted through the crowded terminal as I tried not to faint. Danilo was a rogue Romeo, not just sowing wild oats but baking them into a variety of pies, cakes, and pastas. I asked if he would ever settle down, and he laughed, a deep lupine chuckle flavored with the broken hearts of multiple Guiliettas.

We became friends on Facebook, and for years I watched as partying rounded out his fabulous face and frame. I worried about him, but Danilo's buddy shots of shots with buddies segued into sunset pics with a woman as dazzling as he is. Their smiles shimmer. Two years ago, they married. Their wedding video was a rom com end reel: her heavenly white gown set off her tanned skin and sparkling smile, and Danilo and his friends rode to the ceremony over cobblestoned streets in a posse of gelato colored Vespas. I can't wait to see them peering proudly over the head of a baby who won the DNA jackpot.

But I didn't need to leave the building to experience the literally stunning beauty of Italians.

One night as I took out the trash, I ran into a man on the stairs. By the looks of his impressively braided hat, he was either the pilot of a major airline or the ruler of a minor country. He was magnificently tanned and chiseled and luxuriantly locked, which inspired me to take out the trash several times a day. "Done with that tea bag, hon? I'll take it to the dumpster."

Captain Magnifico wasn't the only jolt to my cardiac rhythm. Our apartment and Giovanna's shared a landing, and one morning as I stood at our open door cradling a full cup of coffee, Giovanna's door opened unexpectedly. Framed in the doorway was her son-in law, Marcello. My brain uttered a long, low whistle. Marcello was over six feet tall; black Italian motorcycle leathers outlined every muscled inch of his slim, lithe body. Ebony curls spilled over his collar onto his shoulders, his sable eyes radiated the warmth of a thousand otters, and a smile illuminated his face like a firework exploding.

Italians must smash a lot of mugs standing in doorways.

But the greatest danger to my heart valves came from the smoldering stranger I called "Fabio on the Balcony."

Chapter 8
Fabio On the Balcony

Our Italian washing machine held two cups of water and one cup of clothes and took four hours to dampen a sock, but I'd gladly trade all my American appliances for a single glimpse of Fabio, the painfully stunning, bronzed Adonis who lived in a nearby apartment building. When I used the clothesline on the roof of our building, I beheld the enclosed terrace that is Fabio's lair.

I could also see Fabio's balcony from our bathroom window. It's hot in Italy, very, very hot. So I needed to keep the bathroom window propped open, and lean out a lot. For, you know, ventilation.

When I wasn't busy maintaining air flow in the bathroom, I was drying our clothes on the roof-top clothesline. To get to the roof, I climbed a medieval iron ladder and flung open the creaking metal door. The sunlight was dazzling as I crossed the searing, pebble-tiled floor to look down upon the oasis that was Fabio's terrace.

I lusted after Fabio's terrace long before I knew who lived there. Fabio's balcony was a cool sanctuary soaked in the warm glow of a Tuscan sunset. The walls were creamy cantaloupe, the floor ochre tile; plants added tropical lushness to the corners. A striped awning and high walls provided protection from Modena's acidic sun, and the terrace doors opened directly into his penthouse apartment. From my perch on the roof, with only scorching tiles to sit on, I longed for the terracotta haven just below.

And then I saw Fabio.

Let us review the splendor that was Fabio: He was impossibly tall, with a broad, tanned chest, a narrow waist, and neatly carved, flat abs. His hair was as thick and dark as polished cherry, with a slight curl that lay along the granite edge of his jaw. He had silken sculpted muscles, and his skin glistened with the lightest sheen of sweat. I had no clear idea of his facial features, because I had only so much time before I started to get faint, and I needed to look at his chest. He looked better than any depiction of any human being I have ever seen.

There have always been people of exquisite beauty—Redford in his *Butch Cassidy* prime, Baryshnikov in tights, Audrey Hepburn in classic *Breakfast at Tiffany's* couture, Beyonce' in anything. Michelangelo's statue of David is brawn infused with purest marble. But Fabio was not on film, on stage, or in a museum. With perilous regularity he appeared in 3D, on a balcony I could see from my apartment.

And he mopped.

I was happily married. I was too old for this. But there he was, a living embodiment of the perfection of Italian design, every time I did the laundry. Every time I hung out the towels, my blood pressure rose, and my heart was deprived of essential fluids. Life is funny. Painfully funny, especially when the cardio infarction started. That usually happened when he leaned over the balcony, but it could flare up when he just strode across the tile.

I was not sure whether insurance covered that.

Fabio had a chaise lounge. It was the natty nautical blue of beach resorts and had a moveable panel to shade the eyes. His chaise was tucked into the coolest corner of the terrace, and I watched him arrange his muscles for repose before he mercifully slipped from view behind the wall. He sunbathed often, to keep his melanin in top form, so sometimes I didn't know he was there until he sat up suddenly, which caused all of my heart valves to slam shut.

I was developing a cardiac condition from hanging out socks.

Cruelly, Fabio upped the ante: he cleaned the balcony *au naturel*. He swept and polished every corner of the cool clay tile. I wondered, as people do, whether he was using a Rasta-wild string mop, or a sponge one that slooowly squeeezed the water out.

He scrubbed the floor in blindingly white briefs. Not that I was looking, but I must say he had bleaching down to a science. Then he watered the plants. He had to bend down really low to water the ivy. He gave that hydrangea a long, slow, drink. And the exertion brought a gloss to his pecs like the sparkle of a precisely cut gem.

I had a fear of heights, and am not mechanically inclined, but I wondered whether wire hangers and paper clips could be assembled into a zip line long enough to reach his balcony railing.

Of course that would be impossible—most of our hangers were made of cheap plastic.

As if the tanning and the mopping were not enough, Fabio installed a patio umbrella, the kind they have at swim-up bars, to shade his table during lunch. How much more of this could I stand? If he sat at the table in his cleaning attire, and poured himself a limoncello, I'd have no choice but to hurtle myself off the roof and try to claw my way onto his balcony. If I missed and dropped all eight floors to the concrete below, would his pouring of citrus liqueur have constituted premeditated homicide?

I mentioned Fabio on the Balcony to my Facebook friends, who demanded photos, which would make me a stalker. Although I was unemployed, that was not in my job description. But because my friends cleverly argued that Signore F was a figment of my imagination, I agreed to take a picture of him.

That weekend, Fabio was joined on the balcony by Sofia. Sofia was clearly not Fabio's sister; I suspected that their home movies were so hot you couldn't watch them without a welder's mask. I didn't want a photo of Fabio with Sofia, and a woman who has a boyfriend like Fabio would notice whether a neighboring apartment has a digital camera, tripods, and a camcorder aimed in their direction. So, I had to wait until Fabio was alone. And then the creepiness of taking a picture slowly dawned on me—looking at Fabio was wrong. I had to stop.

In college, my favorite book was Thomas Mann's *Death in Venice*. I was fascinated and horrified by the tale of Gustav von Aschenbach, an old creep who became obsessed with a beautiful young man. The geezer tried to look younger and more attractive by dying his hair and wearing make-up. As the rancid Romeo decayed, his pursuit of the boy became a greedy but insatiable desire. How hideous. And here I was, writing to Facebook friends about Fabio.

To my credit, my only attempt to enhance my allure was to keep my Costco underwear off the clothesline.

Embarrassed, I had a literary lingerie epiphany: there's no fool like an old fool in sagging skivvies.

So, I renounced my Fabio obsession.

Well, not completely.

The next day, while letting cool air into the bathroom, I glanced outside, and there was Fabio, preparing to sunbathe. The sun buttered his coppery skin, and when he slipped his thumbs beneath the waistband of his briefs, I learned that he was preparing to lay bare the melanin on every inch of Fabio. Every inch of Fabio would be available to anyone willing to rent a helicopter and pay many thousands of euros—a pittance, really—to hover there, above his balcony.

Hold that thought until I get back from the bank.

Chapter 9
Modena

Although our apartment building held many attractions, I knew I needed to face my fears and explore the city.[5]

It took me a while to find Modena, even though we lived there. Except for the Roman-nose-straight Via Emilia, Modena's streets resemble a plate of spaghetti. Wonders awaited at every step, but with no car, limited communication skills, no sense of direction, and the weather an uninviting mix of icy dampness and damp iciness, I was afraid to leave the apartment.

I inherited my lack of a sense of direction from my mother; only 10 percent of the mileage she put on her cherry-red Neon was deliberate, the rest was hopelessly lost meandering. We lived in Rhode Island—the whole state is only 48 miles long and 37 miles wide. Driving 50 miles an hour, a wrong turn can result in several states' worth of backtracking.

Driving in Rhode Island was scary, but even walking in Modena was terrifying. What if I got squashed by a Fiat, or hopelessly lost? My ravenous family would be so relieved at having all the pumpkin and artichoke ravioli to themselves they wouldn't even look for me. Once, returning from an evening visit to a friend's house, I skidded on some wet leaves, and as I slid backward, I feared I would knock myself out on the rock wall behind me. Six months later, I'd regain consciousness in a convent, and be restored to my disappointed family.

It wasn't just that I feared being lost; I was intimidated. The citizens of Modena dress to depress, and the ancient architecture feels like the set of a *Vogue* photo shoot. Italians primp for a paper towel run like I do for dinner at a fancy restaurant. In the piazza, my jeans and black turtleneck lacked pizzaz. Italian fashion is subtle but striking. In the shadow of a medieval wall, a slim woman wore basic jeans and a black coat, but her ballerina flats were scaled in

---

5   Okay, I also didn't want to tell my Facebook friends I was too afraid to leave, spending all my energy leaning out the bathroom window, and running up and down seven flights of stairs on trash runs.

flashing silver that threw off sparks like sunlight skipping across the Aegean. In my TJ Maxx clearance rack wardrobe, I felt more like a rabid rat than a charming country mouse. It's hard to feel like mingling when you look mangy.

When I finally got up the nerve to exit our apartment building, I called Andy to ask how to find the city center. He helpfully explained: "It's along Via Emilia." I reasonably responded: "Where is Via Emilia? And even if I find it, how the hell do I know which way from there?" Ever the geographer, he replied: "Via Emilia goes right by the Ghirlandina Tower."

He was totally counting on having all the pumpkin ravioli to himself.

Despite my fear of absolutely everything, I forced myself to explore Modena.

Walking in town helped me to appreciate the emotional range of idiomatic Italian, from snippets of cellphone conversation often delivered at top volume and with operatic drama. As I turned a corner, an elderly woman in a crisp white coat and a yellow cotton candy 'do threw hard, round syllables into her phone, yelling so loudly that other callers shouting into their cellphones stopped to listen. She bent at the waist and threw out her arms like a Roller Derby queen rounding a curve. Crooking her head like a crow, the Blonde Bomber began jeering at passersby, seeking to incite a small, arthritic knot of senior citizens into starting a rumble. I had no idea what *that* was about, but I veered away; I can't *do* hand to hand combat with septuagenarians.

I wasn't just paranoid, danger was everywhere. With the warmer weather came the bicycles. Elderly people ride them on the coldest days to the market, or just to show off their macho oldness. But on warm days, everyone rides a bike, and it's impossible to avoid them. Along most streets in Modena there are bike paths, usually set back from the street, marked with a protective yellow line to separate the paths from the sidewalks. When you cross a road, if you survive a direct hit by a speeding Fiat, you can always be taken out by a bicyclist; it's good to have options.

Lord knows I tried to avoid collisions. I walked on the sidewalk. If there was no sidewalk, I stuck to the outermost edge of the bike path, following the yellow line. But precautions were useless; bikers found me. Like a camper always in the line of fire of campfire smoke, wherever I went I was directly in the path of a biker.

Waiting at a stop light I'd stay to the right, and as the light changed, wobbling blobs of metal careened toward me. I saw what was coming and couldn't escape: a direct hit from a bike basket to my solar plexus would drop me to the pavement, and as I rolled onto my side, asphalt grinding grit into my eyebrow, I'd form a lumpish speed bump to ensure better traction for multiple tires. As a further insult, from far above the bike seat I'd cringe to hear a petulant, "*Seeeenoooorrraaaaahhhh.*" Because it was always *my* fault.

Without a car, a suit of armor, or a sense of direction, I was petrified of becoming lost in Modena's winding, damp streets. But those streets lead to treasures of lasting beauty. Modena invented sweet vinegar (*aceto balsamico*) that mellows in oak casks under farmhouse eaves for 25 years; a lovely tradition is to start a set of five casks of *aceto* when a baby is born and to present them to the happy couple as a wedding gift. Modena is also home to the headquarters of Maserati, and Ferraris prowl the cobblestone streets. But the most magnificent product of Modena was "Il Maestro."

Chapter 10
Il Maestro

Modena was the home of Luciano Pavarotti. He sang in the choir of the Duomo di San Geminiano, and his funeral, attended by Bono and the Edge, was held there.

Pavarotti died on September 6, 2007. Every September, Modena holds a concert to honor *Il Maestro* in the public square.
We attended in 2009. Piazza Grande was packed; hundreds were seated in the piazza, and hundreds more stood in the streets.

They came to honor a son of Modena, in a cobble-paved square where people have gathered for over a thousand years. Modena is small enough that many of those standing together in the night knew him. As photos of Luciano played against Duomo walls built in the 12th century, the square hummed with pride and respect for *un paesano* who achieved greatness.

The experience was quintessentially European. In Italy, you can stand on ancient stone surrounded by bricks laid civilizations ago and honor someone who will live forever on YouTube. That *is* progress.

Just off the square, an ambulance waited in an alley, doors open and ready for action. I never knew whether the omnipresent ambulances in Italian squares were a sign of the success or of the limitations of socialized medicine. Is the point of the ambulances to demonstrate that the Italian health system provides the ultimate in customer service? Or to whisk away all evidence of failure?

Sure enough, in the opening notes of the concert, we had a casualty. There was no dramatic call for a doctor, merely a muffled yelp from the crowd. The EMTs moved in, surgically removed the concertgoer, and quietly blended into the night. Within 20 minutes, the ambulance was back in position, waiting. Soylent Green is... Italians?

A stage set up in the square held a symphony orchestra. Just in front of us, a short gray man directed the musicians, often in contravention of the conductor on stage, with great passion and energy. He was a priest; at inter-mission, he sang light arias to the evening.

A soprano sang, and a tenor. Their voices soared into the night sky, their instruments as complex and powerful as the symphony. For the first time, I understood how opera feeds the soul. For the first time in a long time, I wanted to hug a priest.

During the concert, color-drenched photos of Pavarotti were splashed against the ancient walls of the Duomo, while a cross-shaped window at the top of the church glowed with a soft and comforting light. At Caffe' Concerto, across the square from the stage, the crowd murmured over drinks and dinner.

The concert didn't begin until 21:15, or after 9 p.m. In Italy, you have to stay up late to experience anything. Reputable restaurants don't open their doors until 7 p.m., the better ones not until 8. Modena has frequent fireworks displays to mark holidays and sports events, many of which were visible from our roof. I missed most of them because they didn't start until after 11 p.m., and I didn't want to celebrate by falling eight stories to my death.

Andy assumed that Sunday night in Italy was like Saturday night at home. But Italians stay out late *every* night of the week. Concerts are held on week-nights, and nothing starts until after 9 p.m. Every Wednesday night during soccer season, the café near our apartment overflowed with locals who flirted and feted until well past two in the morning.

Modena is a town for adults and their pleasures. It's like a perpetual Rat Pack movie, with Sinatra and Dean Martin suavely drinking and smoking all night. And no one ever looked tired, although that could explain the ambu-lances; it had to get to you *sometime.*

As we walked home through the winding streets, I watched breathtak-ingly beautiful Italian women in fabulous shoes, navigate the wobbly cobbles of the sidewalks. In stilettos, they sashayed where Skechers feared to tread. *Belle donne,* laughingly elegant in dresses and heels, glided bicycles across stones that would rattle a yogi. These are the dames who broke Sinatra's heart. And Luciano's, but he made it work for him.

When we got home from the concert, I watched Pavarotti's funeral on YouTube. There was Bono and the Edge, in the Duomo I love, such an odd juxtaposition. This town will never forget Pavarotti. That's beautiful.

You can watch of video of Pavarotti's funeral on YouTube. But better yet, some September 6th, stand in Piazza Grande and watch Il Maestro's towering image flicker against walls built at the edge of time, with a priest who sends his soul to the stars.

Grazie, Il Maestro.

Chapter 11
Market Anxiety

A town that gave the world sweet vinegar, race cars that purr like panthers, and a man who left the musical scale richer with his every note was a tough town to blend into.

A few weeks after we arrived, friends asked if we had settled in, or in a more medicinal term, "adjusted". At home I bought groceries, clothes, went to the post office. In Italy, I tried to do those things, got confused, and retreated into the apartment.

Every step outside the apartment required learning how to navigate a new, incredibly old, country, culture, and language. I grew up with my father's version of Italian, which consisted mostly of swear words ("ma va fangool"). It was fun to realize we used other words "from the Old Country": "pasta fazoo" was pasta *fagioli*, pasta with beans; "skeevie" came from the Italian *schifoso* for disgusting; and "moodandi" (*mutande*) was Italian for underwear. Like other Italian kids from my neighborhood, I studied Italian in school for four years. While I distinctly remember my teacher breezing to the front of the classroom saying, "*Apri il tuo libro alla pagina ventuno,*"[6] when faced with disconcertingly attractive Italians, a million things I wanted to buy, and even basic survival, that particular phrase wasn't helpful.

Every time we left the apartment, we had to learn how to do something we thought we knew how to do, even tasks as basic as buying fruit from a produce vendor. Italian produce sellers display their wares like gems, and just like at Tiffany's, you must ask before handling the merchandise. Italy also has rules about shopping carts, about bagging groceries, buying stamps—and every time I violated a norm, I got a searing look of disapproval, or even worse, the dreaded "*Seeeeenoorrrrrraaaaaahhh…...*"

Of *course* I was afraid to leave the apartment—I was petrified to get *that* look… again. Even going to the supermarket was fraught with unexpected ignorance.

---

6   "Open your book to page 21."

In Colorado, I bought tons of food at the supermarket and hauled it home in my aging minivan, safe from the elements. In Italy we walked to the store, and I was constantly lost. It didn't help that the tiny winding streets, named in honor of thousands of years of Italian heroes, kept the same name for about a block. Via Gobetti became Via Moretti, and in two more blocks, the name, and the direction of the street, changed three more times, while the weather changed from rain to sleet or a foggy combination of both.

When I eventually found the store, the grocery carts were all locked in a clump. To release a cart, you fit a euro coin into a lock on the cart's handle. When you returned the cart, the euro popped out of the lock. But the locks were all different, so you had to figure out how each lock worked, and try not to look like a rube while doing so. And while grabbing someone's empty shopping cart in America is rude, in Italy, it's theft.

In a huge and splendid moral victory, a few weeks after we arrived, I walked alone to the grocery store (take that, Al Gore; if I had lived any more sustainably, I'd have been an actual salmon), got a cart and bought groceries, most of which I recognized, and big finish… paid with my debit card.

But it was plastic pretending to be money, and when I handed it to the cashier, she gave me a sinister calculator box with my card in it; I surmised that I was supposed to enter my PIN. I did, and she seemed satisfied that I had paid for the groceries. Come to think of it, I had no idea *how much* I had paid for the groceries. I was so happy that the charge had gone through that it's possible I paid $200 for eight oranges and some prefab lasagna. But the point here, the good news, was that I finally completed a financial transaction in Italy without the searing public humiliation to which I had become accustomed.

Walking home meant dodging cars that careened toward me at high speed from impossible angles. If the way was clear, I stepped into the road, and AAAAAIIIIIIEEEE!!!! I was inches from Death by Fiat. Most of the cars weren't big enough to take me out gracefully in a cataclysmic bash; there would have been a lot of smearing and unseemly breakage. When the four of us were trapped in an angry nest of buzzing vehicles, I'd shout, "Run, kids! They can't kill us all!" I think Italy added panache to my parenting.

I did adjust to buying groceries at the store. But then I wanted to buy fruit at the fruit stand, bread at the bakery, fish at the fish store. I hadn't adjusted to that yet, and all of those tasks had to be learned. Did I have to weigh the food myself, or did they weigh it for me? What were the words for mussels, for grapes, for that wonderful bread? My fear kept me from opening doors to new wonders.

But who knew that one of the steepest learning curves involved buying stamps at the post office? Melanie, who deciphered mysteries that would have taken me weeks to figure out, told me that a stamp for a letter to the US cost 85-euro cents, and I could buy them at a *tabaccheria*.[7] While the job description for people who work at *tabaccherias* is to sneer at stupid foreigners and their moron questions, I victoriously emerged with three stamps. I had that stamp thing licked!

[Cue up ominous music.]

No, that stamp thing almost licked *me*.

---

7   An Italian word that means: "We sell everything, just not to you."

Chapter 12
Deliver This

When the sun finally sputtered out a candle's worth of warmth, I made a break for it. This was my second stroll to Modena and the first one with a purpose: to buy a bathing suit. We were planning a trip to Tenerife and I couldn't wear jeans and a black turtleneck in a resort pool. This was trickier than it seems. While Italian women have curves as dangerous as Italian roads and wear bikinis into their nineties, I like to keep a layer of Spandex between me and two pregnancies. To find a suit that fit I'd need to shop in the preteen boys' wetsuit department.

I could have tried the local stores, but being trapped in a small shop with a woman with a gorgeous bust who sold bikinis to Italians was way too intimidating. Even better, there was a cheaper option: every Monday in Modena there is an open-air market. They're like our flea markets at home. Miraculously, hundreds of vendors offered amazing deals on everything I wanted: belts, pajamas, shoes. Okay, so there was only one item per size, and some of the boxes looked a little scuffed, like maybe they were stuffed into a foil-lined shopping bag to evade a metal detector, but I did not think for one minute that any of this stuff was stolen. Okay, so I thought that for three minutes, but if I found a one-piece bathing suit in the market, I was happy to let that go. Go, Robin Hood.

The market was somewhere downtown. I headed off on foot. Because it was after 1 p.m., most of the shop windows said "Chiuso." I avoided the old ("old" meaning before Christ—Italians are very serious about old) section of town. It had charmingly winding streets, but if got lost in there I would never make it back out, and the market closed at two.

I couldn't find the market because I was on the wrong street. The right street would have been easily identifiable because the market holds 300 amazing vendors, 800 fabulous Italians, and, if I were lucky, a preteen boys' wetsuit.

I wandered into a stream of college students emerging from class—spiked hair, short jackets, chattering and happy. No wonder they were happy, they looked amazing in bikinis. Confused, I called Andy, who knew where everything was. "How do you get to the open-air market?"

"Take bus number three—it takes you right there."

"I'm already downtown. Now what?"

"Are you north or south of the tower?"

I hate these questions. I couldn't determine direction if I were sitting on the top of the world holding the actual North Pole. But some brain cells fired up, and I figured it out. "I'm north of the tower."

"Go back to the tower. The tower is at Via Emilia. Go to Via Emilia and take a right." I found the tower and took a right. And kept taking it, but there was no market. Along the way there were clothing stores. The crispness of the designs, the richness of the fabric, and the tailoring details were entranc-ing. But there were no bathing suits in the stores, which carried only clothes appropriate to the season, which for me would be a large fuzzy suit like the one Ralphie wore in *A Christmas Story*. Could I find a bathing suit at the street market? Not if I couldn't find the street market.

I passed a mime. He was gorgeous, costumed and painted like an antique playing card. His cheeks were puffy and slid into jowls. His jowls slumped and flared into a magnificent belly. Hmmn, maybe we wore the same size.[8] I wanted to stop and ask him where the market was, but he'd only gesture in Italian, and I was in no mood to translate.

The mime inspired me to write this poem:

I walked to the edge of Italy. I walked so long that some of the little shops were opening up after closing for lunch. That's a bad sign in this country if you want to get home before nightfall.

But look—there's the post office! I had three letters to mail, already stamped with the 85-cent stamps that Melanie told me would send a letter to the US. Efficiently, I dropped the three letters in the mail slot for "out of town" mail. I had fearlessly bought stamps at the *tabaccheria*, and, in a pro move, I

8   I don't recall him having a receptacle that would allow him to be paid for his non-service. He was not only silent, he seemed to reject the very idea of capitalism.

popped my letters into the mailbox. I. Could. Do. This. And now that I was at the post office, I could buy additional stamps! And this one was actually open!

There are a million reasons why at any given moment an Italian post office will be closed. They close for feast days[9] and holidays, or any day after 12:30 p.m. Of course, after 12:30 all post offices should be closed, and they should not open again until the following morning. If you're standing in line at 12:20, they won't serve you anyway, because they are getting ready to close at 12:30.

Sadly, when we first arrived, Andy and I needed to pick up a form that was cruelly available only at the post office. We tried the one near our house, and foolishly waited until afternoon—*Chiuso*. But Giovanna told us that the post office across town was open until 6 p.m. Andy took a bus across town, got to the post office, and it was closed. "*Problemi technicali.*" A car had smashed into the plate-glass windows; weapons were used. The motive was ascribed to robbery, but I suspect that the bandits were just trying to pick up some forms. We tried again the next day and were directed to a big post office in the middle of Modena. "Closed: Union Meeting." The one near Andy's office in Bologna was closed. It was, after all, 12:25.

Freakishly, the post office behind the mime was actually open, so I went inside. I needed more stamps to mail more letters to the US. I had already mailed letters, I knew how to ask for stamps, and I was totally ready for this transaction.

Against the rear wall of the post office was a narrow counter with a long line of hostile postal employees. In this office, the employees did not sit behind bullet-proof glass like other government offices we'd visited. So when a postal employee insisted that, to complete a transaction, you needed to provide seven certified copies of a *blank* piece of paper,[10] it was theoretically possible to fight back.

I noticed that the customers in line were clutching small paper numbers, and that a machine just inside the entrance dispensed three types of numbers based on different types of postal services. The options included paying bills; a list of transactions I couldn't possibly understand; and another list of inscrutable services. Nestled deep within the list of services in option two, I found *francobolli*, (stamps) and pushed the button. I got a number: P288. Now I just had to wait in line.

And wait. Everyone in my postal option line seemed to be holding multiple copies of complicated documents. When their number was called, each customer

---

9   Technically, any day you eat anything in Italy qualifies for a feast day, this enables lots of post office closures.
10   That is actually a thing. See "Permesso, Signore."

heaped their documents on the counter and stood back fearfully. "Providing postal service" means that a postal clerk pokes at the pile, shifts a document or two, and goes away. The clerk directly in front of me had no customer at his counter, and a pile of documents that he occasionally ruffled, listlessly. He was "serving" number P268—this did not bode well. I decided that when buying stamps, the scorn of the *tabaccheria* was preferable to the torturous wait at the post office, and was cheered that I was becoming savvy to the quirks of the Italian mail system.

My number was finally called. The woman who waited on me was finely boned, her long narrow face an etching in thin but firm strokes. As I approached, her slender nostrils flared perceptibly—she was ready for a fight. I asked for 85-cent stamps. Her lips curled into a sneer: Gloves Up.

"Where is it going?" she demanded imperiously. Caligula would have cowered from that sneer.

"The United States," I answered, and I fell into her clutches.

Aaah, an American.

Her Italian moved to warp speed: "Does the letter weigh more than 20 grams?" I had no idea.

"If it's more than 20 grams, You. Need. To. Pay. Extra."

She licked her chiseled magenta lips, infinitely pleased that she could demand for her government that additional bit of payment, as if she would turn the tide for the Italian economy one stamp at a time. She knew full well that Americans are helpless at the metric system and sensed that I did not do serious drugs in college; I had no idea how much 20 grams weighed.

So, I asked, "How much is 20 grams? If it's just a single piece of paper and an envelope, is that under 20 grams?"

"I must weigh it." She was the Empress Josephine, and this bit of Formica counter was her empire.

"But how much does a single piece of paper weigh?"

"I must weigh it. If it is over 20 grams, You. Must. Pay. Extra."

Resisting the impulse to leap over the counter and counteract her reasoning with a little of my own, I slunk away, defeated, muttering more than usual. Is it ME?? If the post office makes a stamp that is used specifically to mail letters to the United States, and the smallest letter to the United States contains only one sheet, is it unreasonable to ask whether a letter to the United States would qualify for the "Single Page Letter to the United States" rate? Could I mail a simple letter without having to stand in an infernal line and wait for Italian postal employees to ignore every document in Italy?

All my adjusting led to more frustration. My clever move to bypass bureaucracy by buying stamps at the *tabaccheria* had failed; by dropping my stamped letters into the mailbox without an official weigh-in, I had affronted the Italian government. Postal employees would breathe on my envelopes, pushing the scale past the magical 20 grams. My three letters, which contained a piece of paper each and cost me almost $4 to mail, would end up in a landfill. And I didn't even find the market, never mind a bathing suit.

No wonder the mime had nothing left to say.

I had adjusted to buying groceries at the store, but had yet to master little shops, and I was incapable of mailing a letter. Had I settled in? If you could settle into quicksand while wearing a suit of iron—if you could settle into a tank full of sharks who have swallowed landmines—then I had settled in.

In those first weeks, I thought my greatest challenge was purchasing stamps, and then I had a new calling: I had to buy a cellphone.

Chapter 13
Phonezilla

I was easy to spot in Modena. I was the only person who was not actually bolted into an iron lung who was not smoking. Also, I had a transcendent smile after the most innocuous transaction. I had to puzzle out how to do the most basic things. For example, keeping a cellphone stocked with voices.

In the US in 2009, you signed up for a calling plan that promised unlimited calls to every nook and cranny of the atmosphere for less than four cents a day. And if you "bundled" phone services, and added cable tv and high-speed internet, you saved so much money that you could quit your job and eat gold nuggets for breakfast. Of course, that was a hideous lie. I bundled and saved, and my phone bills were so high I assumed the phone company had confused me with NASA. But at least I understood the basic theory behind phone operation.

In Italy, it was theoretically possible to get a land line, but to do so involved so much paperwork you'd have an easier time getting permission to reopen Chernobyl as a water park. Everyone, including infants, had a cellphone, and just as you walked down the street in a constant haze of secondhand smoke, you were in a constant buzz of secondhand phone chatter.

But the most ordinary "cellphonese" conversations, *"Dove sei?"* (Where are you) *"Al supermercato"* (At the supermarket) sounded more interesting in Italian than in English, especially when the people chatting were gorgeous and wearing fabulous shoes. And even when a ranting bicyclist was veering toward me, one hand glued to a cellphone and the other wildly waving a cigarette, I was cheered to know I would be ground into the sidewalk in such a charming manner.

I bought our cellphones in a burst of bravado a few weeks after we arrived. When you buy an Italian phone, you buy a microchip that is fueled by euros and keeps track of how much money is still left on your phone. There were different companies, like Vodafone and Wind, and like the choice between a Mac and a real computer, you had to choose one. So, this tech-savvy shopper went online and carefully researched various phone companies to determine the best price and most efficient service. Okay, no: when we first arrived, and I was in a jet-lagged stupor, my friend Melanie, who knows everything, told me to buy a Vodafone with a SIM card. Weirdly, my reptilian brain held on to that information, so in the mall, I found a store that sold Vodafones and SIM cards.

The phone store was full of options. When I found one that seemed capable of incoming and outgoing calls, my techno-needs were met. Anything that this phone could do, including taking photos, it would do in Italian, and I would do in English. If there was any issue with the phone, I Could. Not. Call. For. Assistance... does anyone else see a problem here?

The phone store clerk was young and thickish and mean. She worked in the mall only because there were no jobs available for people who like to stab baby chickens. As I pointed to the Amishly uncool phone I wanted, the clerk's eyes dilated in contempt—that woman was destined for a career at the post office. I told her I wanted a Vodafone and a SIM card, and her lower lip unfurled into a slimy slug of a frown.

"How many euros on the card???!" she demanded.

"Twenty-five," I replied, but her tongue uncoiled and lashed, aiming for the side of my head.

"NO! Only 20, or 50!! NOT 25!!"

"Twenty, then," I said, wishing I had a saltshaker to discourage further displays of the inside of her lip.

She put the phones on the counter, and I gave her my debit card; those were the heady days just before my card stopped working. She asked for identification, so I showed her my Colorado license.

Check.

"*Codice fiscale?*" That was my tax code number, which the Italian government considered so private that I needed to show it to use a public bathroom.

Check.

"Passport?"

Check mate.

Why, of *course* I was carrying my passport. I also carried the hospital bracelet from the day that I was born, just in case I needed to buy electronics.

"I *must* see your passport." Her lower lip was doing a little happy slug dance, and I wondered if DDT was still available in stores.

"I don't have it with me," I said, and she swept the phones off the counter. They were the size of thimbles, so it wasn't that dramatic of a gesture. But my failure to complete yet another simple task settled like coffee grounds into the chambers of my heart. Why does every transaction in Italy take 14 trips and 27 pieces of identification?

I slogged back home for my passport, collected some mitochondria samples just in case, and trudged back to the mall. When I was finally allowed to buy the phones, I fired them up with 20 euros of conversation each. To this day I have no idea how much it costs to make a call, either locally or otherwise; I used the phone only to chat with my bank about how they couldn't send me either my debit card or an email. The first 20 euros lasted about a month, and 70 calls to my bank. When the euros ran out, the phone stopped working, and I had to recharge the SIM card.

I had no idea how to do that, so I took the bus back to the mall and got the wench who sold me the phones to do it. But I was looking for love in all the wrong places; I was like an orphaned duckling who had imprinted on a piranha. I brought cash, my passport, my *Codice Fiscale*, and a salt packet for self-defense. Phonezilla recharged the phone, but she was contemptuous of my pathetic dependence and my mixed metaphors; I needed to learn how to charge my own phone.

When the phone ran out after another month and another 70 calls to my bank, I was determined to figure it out for myself.

I knew that *Ricarica*, "recharge" cards looked like credit cards and were sold at the grocery store and in phone stores, but I watched the phone store clerk install the microchip, and I didn't understand how a plastic card fit into the microchip scenario. Technology is not my strong point, but I was desperate to avoid Phonezilla.

One day I noticed that tabaccherias also advertise phone recharge services. No wonder the clerks of tabaccherias are so full of themselves—they do all the real work of Italy. Tabaccherias sell the tax stamps required to initiate an application for residence documents, and they sell postage stamps without the bone marrow sample required by the post office. They recharge cellphones. And they sell cigarettes, which is how all these gorgeous people fit into all that fabulous clothing. All that's left for tabaccherias to do is to sell coffee. If tabaccherias sold coffee, the rest of Italy could shut down completely. That must be why it's fine with Italians when it so frequently does.

I entered the *tabaccheria*, asked for a *ricarica*, and the shop clerk asked for my phone number. I had written out the number and taped it to the back of the phone; I could have been mute in that town and gotten along just fine. I gave the clerk 50 euros and watched carefully. Oooh, he called the phone service and told *them* to charge the phone. The plastic cards at the supermarket worked the same way; there was a bar code on the back. You called the company, entered the numbers, and the phone was recharged.

I emerged with this new knowledge and a radiant grin. All of the brilliant smiles in Italian art were captured at the moment the artist's model was able to complete a simple task, like successfully buying a potato, or an 85-cent stamp. I'll bet that the *Hallelujah Chorus* was written after Handel successfully recharged his Italian cellphone. Completing a minor transaction in Italy is cause for a monumental celebration.

A cappuccino is a great place to start.

Although I couldn't buy stamps to send a letter to the US, with a cellphone I could reach the world! And then, on January 20th, I lost access to my bank account. For three hilariously excruciating months.

Chapter 14
Carded

To celebrate Obama's reelection, I assembled supplies for an inauguration soiree. At an outdoor flower stand, I bought roses to wrap in ribbon and present to everyone in our apartment building. In a horrific bit of foreshadowing, while I was paying for the roses, I dropped a coin—a $2 euro coin worth almost five bucks—and it rolled and rolled until it disappeared into an inexplicable hole in the pavement. It wasn't a drain, or an officially sanctioned aperture, it was just a hole in the road that portended my impending financial ruin.

At the market I heedlessly heaped ribbon and some party food onto a cashier's conveyor belt and handed her my debit card. She swiped it and said it didn't work. How embarrassing. I handed her my backup debit card—that didn't work, either. It was dinner time, there were people behind me in line, and they were disgusted with the stupid American who failed at shopping.

No problema. I scurried to the store's ATM, inserted my card, put in my PIN, and the machine asked quite civilly how money much I wanted. As I was reaching for the cash, the ATM screen flashed: *Carta di Credito Rifiutata*, (Credit Card Refused). Followed by: *Carta di Credito Detenuta* (Credit Card Detained). Card rejected? Card DETAINED?????!! The machine ARRESTED my debit card?? My groceries were already rung up, there were hungry Italians behind me, and I not only couldn't access cash, I didn't even have a bankcard. What???!!! I went back to the cashier and tried to explain, but she was registering boredom bordering on hostility.

The ATM ATE my card??!! The situation called for some humanitarian assistance, but that was not in the cards. The cashier called over the manager, who rolled two glazed eyeballs rimmed by perfectly mascaraed eyelashes, and started putting my groceries away.

I had already moved beyond embarrassment to shock. When I packed for Italy, I didn't bring any credit cards, because, without a job, I couldn't pay the money back. So, Miss Responsible brought only debit cards that accessed money I had thriftily deposited in my checking account. But 20 days into our year in Italy, neither of my debit cards worked, and one of them had been confiscated.

I was flummoxed. Now what??

Phew: I called Melanie. She had lived in Italy for years and could fix any logistical problem, in several languages, over the phone. Melanie growled, "These people will not help you unless you insist. Give the phone to the store manager, and I'll talk to her."

There was a peevish conversation involving vicious vowels and aggrieved gestures that eventually ended with the store manager telling Melanie the name of the bank that owned the ATM. From 100 miles away in Milan, Melanie figured out which company serviced that specific ATM at that grocery store. Melanie should be in charge of everything, especially the international banking crisis.

I stomped home to call my Colorado bank.

"How can I get my card back?" The perky bank employee cheerfully explained that my debit card had expired, and it wouldn't work anyway. WHAT? Then Melanie called and said the Italian bank had sent a guy to the store to retrieve my card from the ATM.

I trudged back to the store, and an amiable ATM technician opened the machine and gave me back my card. I asked him to wait while I tried the other card, so I could buy groceries. I put in the card, entered the PIN and: "Card rejected. Card detained."

DETAINED? What IS it with this country? You could rob a bank and they wouldn't confiscate your card. You could pull an armed robbery, do hard time, get out of prison, stroll directly to an ATM, and the bank would pump out a stack of fresh euros with a reassuring, "We missed you, here's your cash."

I was having an international banking crisis; the Italian banking system cut off access to my American money. Now what?!

Chapter 15
Don't Bank on It

Because of my unbalanced relationship with my American bank, we attempted to bond with an Italian one. We needed to open a bank account, but first we needed to open a bank. At the branch Giovanna recommended, there was a button next to the door, and a sign that said: *Disoirdositiri Fantfiodefi*.[11]

To enter the bank, we had to wedge ourselves into what looked like a cross between a pneumatic bank tube and a Star Trek transporter, only smaller. Once we were sealed like a checking deposit into the tube, the doors slid shut, and then we pressed buttons that would either direct Scotty to beam us up or suck us upwards until we were distributed somewhere else in the bank. Encased in the clear cylinder, we pushed various buttons to no avail and for several mystifying minutes remained trapped in the tube, in full view of the bank employees behind the counter.

Eventually the tellers relented and slid open the door.

The bank was tiny—a counter, three tellers, and two visitor chairs. A door marked *Directore* was firmly shut. The tellers were very slim, in that Italian way that lets you know they were wearing exquisite shoes. We sat down to wait. Giovanna had given us the card of someone at the bank, Filippo, so I asked to see him. But while we were talking, Filippo had escaped outside with the guy who let us into the bank; they were speaking with great animation about the door's keypad. I could see that because I could see everything that happened outside the bank through the floor to ceiling glass windows.

The other teller, Teller Numero Due, said Filippo would be back soon. Or that's what I thought he said. He spoke in very rapid Italian, with vowels that were as clipped and as thin as he was. Then he waited on other customers. Warmly, with rich, fat vowels that puffed and billowed across the counter like

---

11   I just made that up, but whatever the sign actually said, it meant: "We are all watching you trying to get into the bank, and laughing at you."

clouds of affection, while we waited for Filippo. Or the end of international banking, which for me had already started.

Hovering over Filippo's desk, and in full view of the entire bank, was a large screen that showed the security camera's view of the front door, to let the tellers know if someone was trapped inside the tube. Or you could just look outside; outside and inside were separated only by clear glass walls. No wonder they couldn't see us.

We festered in our cheap plastic chairs. Filippo came back in, ignored us, and waited on another customer who came in after we did. When Filippo finished with that customer, he disappeared without a word. Was he on break? Did he know we were there to see him, was he the right person? The other teller ignored us. We ignored each other. More people arrived. Teller Numero Due adored each of them, answered their medical questions, organized their digital photos, made reservations for their summer vacations, gave them tea and cookies with personalized frosting. Us, nothing. Filippo had skipped town, changed identities, and we were left to watch Teller Due bond with all of Modena.

Finally, Filippo returned. He was pleasantly glossy and crisp in an impeccably tailored suit. He called us by name, said Giovanna had called about us and that he was already working on opening our account. He requested a few things—four million pieces of identification, a kidney, exculpatory notes from our third-grade teachers, and lots of money. He said he'd draw up the papers and call us when we could come back and sign them. Although his bank had almost all of our money, until the papers were signed, we were wrong to expect to use any of it ourselves. If we wanted to make withdrawals, or to obtain an ATM card, they'd need a few more days, maybe some more documents, possibly a cornea; it was gauche to pry.

We chatted amiably about how *of course* we couldn't take our money out of our account, and we all agreed that we should check back in a few days to see if anything had changed. Since we were now practically related, I asked about my debit card. I inserted it into their ATM, put in my PIN, and: "Card detained."

I was starting to get *crankone*. During a global banking meltdown, everyone in the world had fistfuls of credit cards they couldn't possibly pay off and was able to rack up mountains of debt, but I wasn't allowed to touch a dime of my own money. How was this my life?

Filippo called someone who identified the problem and broke it to me gently: I had used my card too many times. "Too many operations," he explained. I had no idea what that could possibly mean, but I loved that he actually tried to help. And I HAVE to say, Filippo was completely adorable in that Italian way that makes you forgive them everything, especially if it involves sex or cappuccino. Sex was out, so I was totally ready for coffee.

I called my American bank again, and this time I was told that both of my debit cards were cancelled, and they had mailed me a new one, on December 29th.

Wait. WHAT? The week of December 20th, before I left Colorado, I had called my bank to say: "I'm leaving for Italy on December 31st, and I'm going to live in Italy for a year."

Snippily, the customer servicer responded, "When were you planning to tell us that?"

"I'm telling you now," I snipped right back.

So, although I had told my bank, "I'm leaving for Italy December 31st and I won't be back for a whole year," two days before I left, on December 29th, FirstBank wisely decided to cancel my bank card and send a new one to my Colorado address. The two debit cards I took to Italy had the same number, so both cards went kaput on January 20th, just before I set my inauguration-fest purchases on the conveyor belt at the grocery store. I didn't need high-end Italian shopping options like Ferraris to drive me to financial ruin, I could do that just by buying snacks.

Weeks later, I still didn't have a debit card, and our Italian bank was still deciding whether to let us access our own money. You would think that I only had to call my American bank and they would send me a new card immediately, and all would be fine. That would be wrong. Three insanely frustrating months wrong.

It wasn't that I didn't have any money; the Italian bank thought I had performed too many operations. And my American bank refused to send me a new card because… their interest rate was low? Ten years later, I still do not know why. And in the kind of thing that happens only **to me**, unlike everyone else in my family, I was unable to receive mail.

Chapter 16
Buzz Off

More than a month after the ATM fiasco, my sister emailed that she sent me a package. Calendars, for the kids. She sent it by FedEx and expected delivery by Friday. I laughed: I DO NOT RECEIVE PACKAGES. Perhaps the Italian postal service had been reading my blog and was taking revenge for certain mean things someone may have said, entirely in jest, there.

Or maybe the mime spilled the beans after he heard me muttering outside the post office. Never trust the word of a mime.

In early January, a friend threw our Colorado mail into a box and sent the package through the US Postal Service. There were 800 different options for the delivery of packages, and all but two of them provided a means to track delivery. My friend chose an impressive sounding option, something like "International Premium Priority Delivery She'll Get This You Betcha." But not realizing my bank card was inside, she didn't choose an option that added "She'll Get This You Betcha And She Can Track the Package." By the middle of February, a month and a half after she mailed it, the package hadn't arrived.

Not that we didn't receive other mail. Andy ordered books, and days later, snug little packages were nestled comfortably in his hand. The kids ordered enough Legos to build a plastic metropolis—they were delivered so fast you could hear the wind whistling inside the box. But no mail for me. Why didn't *I* get mail?

I was seriously considering having a talk with that mime.

Even while I had adjusted to basics like shopping for groceries and not getting lost in our apartment lobby, mail delivery remained a frustrating enigma. We had a slim metal mailbox that opened with a key. Theoretically, if we received something too big to fit in the mailbox, *Il Postino* (the Postman) would ring the buzzer on the outside of the building, and we could go downstairs to the lobby to pick it up.

The buzzer was attached to a phone on the wall. The first time the buzzer rang, I was alone in the apartment and had no idea what was making a sound like the war cry of a thousand rabid mosquitos, and, afraid of what that meant, I ignored it. Was that my package? I'll never know.

The second time the buzzer rang, we realized we needed to answer the buzzer using the phone. I lifted the receiver, said, "*Pronto*" and realized— *Ohhhh...* the buzzer meant someone was calling from the lobby. But the lobby was seven flights down; given the asthmatic elevator or a having to run down seven flights of stairs, by the time I reached the mailbox, whoever buzzed would be long gone. What an excellent system.

Another day, there was a distant buzz, and Giovanna knocked on the door. Il Postino had given her a package for Andy. Books, that he ordered by phone— life was so easy for him. Another time there was a buzz, I didn't get there in time, but there was a receipt in the mailbox that said there was a package waiting at the main post office in Modena. Andy brought the slip to the post office and *ba da bing*—he had another box of books.

I think Andy knew more about that mime than he was saying.

Many days there were buzzes, and packages or receipts for Andy or the kids, neither of whom desperately needed to access their freaking bank accounts. But there was no package, no bank card, not even a slip in the mailbox, for me.

After a month of waiting for the box of mail, I thought my bank owed me something. Like my bank card. I called my bank and asked if they would cancel the old card and FedEx me a new one. The bank was suitably sorry for the mix-up, deeply apologetic, and ready to get to work to set things right.

Actually no, the customer service person was churlish, like the banking crisis was my fault and this missing debit card business was just another of *my messes* that *they* had to clean up, using bailout money provided by my tax dollars. No remorse there.

When I asked for a new bank card, the clerk said the bank would FedEx it to me, but I must be available to sign for it, or Fed Ex would just send the card back to the United States. Since the US Post Office package with my new debit card had never arrived, I was determined to actually receive the bank card; I asked her to send me the FedEx tracking number so I would know when the card would arrive. If I knew when it will be there, I could be there to sign... was this not a reasonable request?

"No, I can't give you the tracking number."

"Why can't you give me the tracking number?" I asked in a clipped British accent, as if this were a Monty Python episode.

"That's not my department. I just ask for the card, but the ATM department orders it, and they don't give me the tracking number."

Oh, what a delightfully reasonable explanation.

"Where is the ATM department?" I inquired, trying to help this process along.

"Across the room. But she's not here."

"Can you leave her a note?"

"We work different hours."

I thought I would grind my molars into dust, just to keep myself from uttering a piercing scream. "Would it be possible for you to email the ATM department, with a *cc* to me, so I know that you have asked for the tracking number, and then she can email the number to me?"

"No, I'll just ask her on Monday. You'll have to call back."

How dare I ask her for an email? It was an outrageous plan, an audacious attempt to throw myself into the gaping jaws of finance and stop its relentless consumption of the expensive and limited minutes left on my phone card.

Of course, I had to call back on Monday, and my voice on this call was so high and so tense that I sounded like I had inhaled a tank of helium. I asked again, as patiently as erosion grinds a continent into sand, whether the tracking information for the FedEx delivery of my bank card could be emailed to me. And Ryan, my customer service representative du jour, promised that he would. And he did. His email with the tracking information stated that delivery would occur on Wednesday, February 12th by 8 p.m.

That morning, a horde of mosquitos shook the buzzer phone: it's Postino time!! I grabbed the phone, said, "*Un momento*," and flew down the steps. There was no time to grab keys, or shoes, so I left the apartment door open, threw on a coat, and when I got down the seven flights, Mr. Postman was already across the street. On his motor scooter, with his little basket of mail.

I called to him: "*Postino*?!" then realized the door to the building was closing, which would leave me outside in the cold without shoes. I ran back to prop it open. He scooted over, but I had no idea what to say, so I pointed to our nameplate on the outer door. He replied, *"Dadododoaodososdsoda sododoeieiodod-soidosiodileralla."* Well, now we were getting somewhere.

I thought he was saying that he didn't have the package, but he left a receipt in the box and we could take that to the post office. That made sense, he drives a little motorbike and there was no room for packages. But when I got back inside and opened the mailbox, it was empty. No package, no receipt. Fortunately, that little encounter didn't leave me standing on the sidewalk in my socks. But I had no idea what the hell he buzzed me for, unless it was just to ensure that I got locked out of our building.

Or was the buzzer from FedEx? Who knows? Yes, dear God yes, I did leave the apartment, for 45 minutes. *Elvis left the building.* I practically ran to the grocery store, then ran back with three heavy bags. It was wrong, but I had no food, and Elvis would have supported me on that.

While I was gone, did FedEx deliver my bankcard? If they got no response to the evil buzzer, did they send my card back to the United States? When it landed with a plastic *thwip* on the desk of the ATM Department, customer servers would shake their heads and say, "We *knew* she was a bad seed." Then they'd shred my card and spend my portion of the taxpayer bailout on a luxe retreat to celebrate their dedication to the art of customer service.

Or perhaps FedEx delivered my card to the mime. All day he stood on his wooden box, in the same position, never took a break, and no one suspected that he was secretly working for the post office. And FedEx. To keep me quiet?

My sister sent me calendars, and I hoped she sent them for 2011; 2010 wasn't looking good for package delivery.

Chapter 17
Going Postal

Great news! In late February, the long-awaited package of Colorado mail arrived!! We were all sitting around the apartment when the *Postino* rang. We flew down the steps, he gave us the package, and we all gave him a grateful wave as our selfless public servant scootered off... okay, no.

The Postino rang, we flew down the steps, and found a slip in the mailbox? No again.

The Postino rang, and we found the package safely perched atop our mail slot?

Notto.

Here is what really happened: one morning we ran out of bottled water, so Andy went out to buy more. When he opened the lobby door to the street, he found the box of mail propped up against the *outside* of our building. The Postman *Always* Rings Twice? No, not really. Sometimes the Postino doesn't ring at all. He rings if he doesn't have a package, he rings if he's not going to wait for you, sometimes he rings just for the pure thrill of knowing that by pushing that little round harbinger of hell, he could make me run down seven flights of stairs, babble incoherently, and quite possibly get locked out of the building. But the package that I'd been waiting for, for two months? Why tell me? Leave it outside, I would have found it eventually. Or... was it meant for the... MIME????

Lying forlornly in the box of mail was my debit card. But it was long expired; I had given up hope of ever receiving this package, and I had cancelled this card a month before, in the vain hope of getting a new one. I was so disappointed I couldn't even open the envelope. I left it, in its pristine paper coffin, with its raised and hopeful little numbers pushing against its thin cold shroud. It was sad, really. While all the other debit cards were gleefully sliding into ATMs and card machines, financing martinis, mochachinos, and Maseratis, that little card expired before it got a chance to pay for a single stamp, if that even were an option. My card was dead, and I had killed it, because I didn't trust that a package that was two months late would ever arrive.

I'm afraid I'll have to do something about my paranoia.

And what of my new debit card, to replace the one I assassinated? The bank was supposed to send it by FedEx, and—by sheer force of will—I had obtained its tracking number!! The FedEx website started tracking the card's meandering progress through Europe, which made the advance of the Allies in World War II look speedy by comparison. The card cleared Customs in Paris, sauntered on to Palermo with some two-day book orders, lingered for a cappuccino with an overnight garment delivery on the outskirts of Milan, and was malingering in Crespellano, a suburb outside of Bologna. Thank God it wasn't a box of fresh squid.

From the looks of my card's FedEx itinerary, it wouldn't arrive before we went back to the US in December, and definitely not before we left for Tenerife in March. If I weren't there to sign for the envelope when it was delivered, FedEx would return it to the States.

So, Miss Overly Controlling Person emailed FedEx and asked them to hold the envelope until we returned. Much to my relief, FedEx emailed me a copy of my request. Of course, FedEx didn't tell me it would *hold* the package, but they helpfully let me know that I had *asked* them to. Customer service wasn't dead, but it had such a phlegmy, hurlish kind of a flu that you didn't want to get close enough to ask for anything.

I also emailed my bank to let them know that I requested that the FedEx not be returned to the US. Because if the card were returned to the bank, they'd take a meat cleaver to it. Of course, FirstBank—who had toiled on my behalf to the point of martyrdom, it was embarrassing, really—responded that they couldn't stop FedEx from returning the card to the US. After three months of increasingly unhinged emails and phone calls, I had an old card that didn't work, and no idea what happened to the new one that did.

Chapter 18
Are We There Yet?

By March I was starting to crack. I had been waiting since February 12th for FedEx to deliver my debit card. Lord knows I tried. I tried to contact them by email, (itmaster@fedex.com), by phone (1800-Go-FedEx doesn't work in Italy), and I got no response.

FedEx was like my personal mime: I waved, got in its face, and no expression rippled the serene surface of the purple and orange logo on its package tracking website. The tracking report said that my package was nestled safely in the local facility in Crespellano, but none of my increasingly frantic emails convinced FedEx to ask the Crespellanians to let me have it.

Should I go there myself? If I hurt myself doing something socially unacceptable, like taking out a Crespellanian, would I be covered by socialized medicine?

But I couldn't go to Crespellano. I was afraid to leave the house, because if I missed the delivery, FedEx would send the card back to the US, and I'd have to start the whole hellish process over again. Did anyone ever ask agoraphobics whether they're actually just waiting for a FedEx? It's worth a shot.

Thank God for email. It gave me something to do while I waited. A friend emailed me a link to an article in *The New Yorker*. I once read a *New Yorker* article about Kawasaki Disease, a rare illness that can cause permanent heart damage in children. Several years later, Annalise developed those same symptoms: high fevers, red palms, red feet, red lips, red eyes. The whites of Annalise's eyes were bright red, and her eyelids were rimmed in purple; she looked like a vampire, but I knew she wasn't Transylvanian, she was dangerously ill. The redness was caused by a swelling of all her arteries, including those in her heart and her brain. But seven doctors, including several at a children's hospital, told us that Annalise had "just a virus."

Because I had read about the symptoms, I knew it wasn't just a virus.

Because of a *New Yorker* article, I knew that Annalise needed treatment within seven to ten days. She got it on day five.

That article saved my daughter's heart; I will subscribe to that magazine for the rest of my life. Hell, I'll subscribe from the grave. In the crematorium, while the flames are licking at my feet and I'm finally warm enough for the first time in my life, even though I'm dead, I will welcome my weekly issue of *The New Yorker*. If I'm in Colorado, my postman can just toss it onto my burning pyre on his daily rounds.

But I couldn't subscribe to a magazine in Italy. I couldn't get a single package delivered to me a single time. A *weekly* magazine? I'd see the Postino in hell before I saw a single issue, but only if they let you bring contact lenses to hell, otherwise I wouldn't have known it was him. But if you could bring contacts, and I did see him in hell, I was totally going to say something mean. "Do you think men who drive scooters are compensating for something?!"

It was such a diabolically perfect plan, unless they don't let you bring contacts. That *would* be hell.

Because getting a magazine in my Italian mailbox was not an option, I emailed *The New Yorker* about subscribing online, and I got the usual "don't call us, and we probably won't call you" customer service response:

From: The New Yorker
Subject: Thank you for contacting Customer Service (KMM29936079I103L0KM)
To: agelfuso@rocketmail.com
Date: Wednesday, February 25, 2009, 9:57 AM
We have received your e-mail inquiry. Your message has been submitted to a customer service representative and will be taken care of as soon as possible. Please do not reply to this message. Thank you for contacting The New Yorker.

A normal person, who was not trapped in an apartment waiting for a FedEx that will never come and thinking of mean things to say in hell to a postal employee, would not even *read* a "Do Not Reply" email. But a person trapped in an apartment waiting for a FedEx that will never come is not a normal person. Isolation was taking its toll, and I come from a long line of lunatics. My family has a history of insanity like other families have a history of cowlicks and investing in public utilities. This cracking thing was to be expected, so of course I responded:

Dear New Yorker,

Thank you for sending me an acknowledgement of my email. I treasure the push-me-pull-you dance of customer service emailers the world over: "We grovel at your feet, but don't make eye contact."

Every Customer Service email says:

"Please don't reply to this message."

Why not, I ask? You thanked me for contacting you, and thoughtfully assigned my message number KMM29936079I103L0KM. I promise not to reveal my bra size, and I'm not expecting an invitation to the employee appreciation brunch, but what on earth should prevent me from replying, just one time, to one of these Do Not Reply messages?

HA! I responded anyway! It's liberating, really. And my bra size is Double D. No, it's not. Soylent Green is... none of your business.

If you reply, I won't even look.[12]

Andrea Gelfuso

No really, I sent that. I used to be a lawyer. I solved problems. Big ones, involving national parks, and oil and gas operations, and laws with so many words in them that I hoped someone from CliffsNotes would get elected to Congress.

And I taught environmental law to college students. I explained the Clean Air Act in three hours so that it was just as easy to understand as the directions for microwave popcorn. And if at the end of class my students had little puffs of smoke coming out of their heads, and smelled kind of buttery, I blamed Congress.

Sadly, I used to *do* things. But in Modena I waited for FedEx, sent insane emails to customer service, and I didn't even *have* a microwave.

I had no access to cash, and had a hostile relationship with FedEx, the postal systems of two countries, and the entire banking industry. Worse, our family didn't yet have the legal right to remain in Italy, because we lacked an essential document, a *Permesso Di Soggiorno*, which sounds festive right until you're deported for not having one.

---

12   In a triumph of the human spirit, several years later I was actually published in *The New Yorker*. It's a letter to the editor about pesticide regulation, but I was in there. https://www.newyorker.com/magazine/2014/03/10/the-mail-22

Chapter 19
Permesso, Signore

Although we had a visa that let us stay in Italy for one year, we also needed a *Permesso Di Soggiorno*, a residence permit, which possibly entitled us to free medical care, but definitely entitled us to taxation. That seemed like a wash, but without it, we could be deported. To get the Permesso, we had to go to 400 obscure government offices that were usually closed, take numbers that were never called, and wait in line until we finally realized that what we actually needed was a form from the post office.

Since the post office was open only 14 minutes a week, it took another month to obtain a copy of the form. Then we needed a *marca da bollo* (a cool sticker that shows we paid taxes to process the form) from a tabaccheria, and a copy of every page of our passports, including the *blank* ones. Especially the blank ones.

We had to take the completed Permesso form to the post office. A postal employee (who had probably heard about the stamp debacle from the mime) scrutinized our documents, then sneeringly insisted we needed certified copies of the *blank* pages of our passports. When we finally provided a sufficiently large stack of blank paper, the postal official demanded 70 euros. Then he stomped his rubber stamp over everything on top of the counter, including our application, his credit card machine, and all the fingers of Andy's left hand. In the grand finale, he gave us a pile of receipts to certify that we had completed a huge transaction for no apparent reason. The end goal of this application process was a letter that set up a time to meet with... dun dun DUUUNNNN... the *Questura*.

The Questura is a cross between police headquarters, Italian Immigration, and the corporate offices of the Wicked Witch of the West, Inc. We were supposed to meet with the Questura within eight days of our arrival in Italy. The fact that it took a month just to find an open post office and another month to get an appointment didn't weigh heavily on the conscience of the Questura. But we started out knowing that we were already so far past the eight-day deadline that we were probably going to be deported no matter what we did next.

All fear the Questura.

Expats who live in Italy simply advise: "Humble yourself."

About a month after we submitted the form to the post office, we received a letter from the Questura which set the time for our appointment. Mine was for 9:48 a.m. on March 2nd, Andy's was for 10:48. I assumed that I would spend an hour being questioned closely by brutes who would demand my documents and ask me to sing songs with a Mussolini-related theme. (Would train songs work?) I dreaded the meeting and wondered how I would pack for deportation. Would they give me toothpaste suitable for sensitive teeth? Would FedEx forward my bank card to a rendition facility?

On the morning of our dreaded appointment, Andy woke me by fluttering the letter from the Questura in my face. "This letter says we need to bring four photographs." Andy delights in delivering these news bulletins to me when it is far too late for me to do anything about them. For example: "Andrea, the train derailed about 40 miles back. It has now left the tracks and we are plunging into the ravine."

"Why, thank you for the update, Hon. I'll get out my grappling hook and crash helmet."

For this particular crisis, it was 7:18 a.m., and we needed to be at the Questura, with eight photographs, in less than... oh, you do the math, I had to get dressed. In the United States, I know where to get passport photos: you hop into the car, walk into a drug store, and in half an hour you have photos of your least-attractive parent.

But in Italy, the drug stores don't *do* passport photos; you can't even buy saline. For saline, I had to go to an optician. We were four photos away from an Alitalia flight to nowhere and didn't have a clue where to get them. A knot of horror bunched every nerve at the back of my neck: we were going to be deported, and I didn't even know if there was an Italian version of Guantanamo.

So of course, I called Melanie, who knows everything. She said, "The photo machines are at train stations, bus stations. Bring change. You'll be fine."

We got to the train station, found the machine: "Fun Fotos." Apparently, the Fun Foto booth also doubles as a urinal. Eight euros later, smelling slightly like ammonia, we had our photos. I assumed we weren't supposed to smile, and the acrid odor had curdled my moisturizer. The resulting pictures were even more horrifying than usual; I would have been better off with a stock photo from a zombie movie. If I were the Questura, I would deport me just for looking so bad.

As we waited with morning commuters for the bus to the Questura, an elderly man was scanning the crowd around him like a boxer sizing up his opposition. His frowning face was crushed into itself like a hand crumpling a piece of paper. When he looked at me, the fist of his face clenched tighter. "Alright, I *know* I look bad!! I'm only here for a year!" I wanted to shout, but our bus was leaving.

When we reached the office of the Questura. I expected the jagged spires of the Wicked Witch of the West's castle, but it was a nondescript brick building. Still, you could see where the flying monkeys get in and out of the upper windows. Huge block letters proclaimed our doom: "QUESTURA." Surrender, Dorothy.

We walked into a large room, took a number, and got in line. Okay, no, because there were no numbers, no lines. The crack team of efficiency engineers at the Questura had designed a perfect service delivery system. On the wall at the back of the room there was an electronic number board. But it was turned off. On the left, near the electronic board, a clump of people sat in plastic chairs. On the right there was a wall with a single open doorway. Through the doorway you could see a counter: the lair of the dreaded Questura.

With no numbering system, and no line, around 40 people of many nationalities waited, in various states of terror and hopelessness. Most of them were standing by a doorway that was swollen with people. The room was silent, but it hummed with anxiety in multiple languages. We took a place at the back of the mob, but a kind man with soft sienna eyes motioned to Andy that we should move to the front.

We stood at the open door but had no idea what to do.

It was 9:45 and my appointment was in three minutes, but there was no indication that anyone knew I was there or cared. Through the doorway you could see that the customer service counter was shielded to the ceiling by bullet-proof glass, a sure sign that the customer is always wrong. There were four *sportelli*, (windows) but only three officials to serve a crowd that swelled as we stood there.

Behind the officials there were open stacks of files on shelves. I wondered if those were the files of the people about to be deported, and if my file was in that stack. But there was no one to ask, and no signs to tell us what to do. I watched and listened, hoping for a clue.

The official in *Sportello Uno*, a man with a marvelous Mediterranean face in shades of olive and deep brown, spoke English. At his window was a sturdy

Black woman who spoke English and Italian. Sportello Uno asked for a series
of documents, and she fed him a steady supply that seemed to satisfy him. But
eventually he hit on a document that she didn't have. "*A casa,*" she said—at her
house—and she was punted from the window. "Come back tomorrow."

In *Sportello Due*, directly in front of me, was an attractive official with dark
eyes and a stern face. His victim seemed to have completed the process; he was
asked to provide a photo and a fingerprint.

To the right, in *Sportello Tre*, was a snub-haired balding blonde with a distinct
Fascist flair. His default face was set on grimace, and he got nastier with each change
of expression. I wondered if we could swap his more attractive ID badge photo for
mine in my application. But he was working some poor soul over and yelled over
every document; I sensed he wasn't open to questions of a personal nature.

While we were standing in front of the doorway, trying to figure out
how to proceed, Sportello Due indicated that I was supposed to step toward
the windows. When I hesitated, I got an extra flurry of a wave. The Fates
were against me: at that moment, the only available official was Sportello
Numero Three, at the Gates of Hell.

Fearing deportation for being late for my appointment, or for having
a bad photo, or just for breathing, I stepped toward Signore Scary, and
held out my Questura letter like I was offering raw meat to a rabid tiger.
He grabbed the letter and exploded with fury, then shouted, "Outside!
Wait!!" He put the letter in a stack on the counter in *Sportello Numero Quattro*.
Sportello Numero Four was the filing system for the entire operation: a pile
of papers held down by half of a painted coconut.

I stepped back in terror. This was going well so far. "*I've been working on
the raaaaillroad...*" Signore Scary bellowed something, apparently a name. He
had a microphone directly in front of his face, but he didn't use it. His voice
was loud but impossibly muffled, the sound of a pillowcase of rocks being
thrashed against bricks.

The doorway, only three feet wide, was cut into an otherwise unbroken plaster wall. The waiting people were fanned out beyond the doorway,
behind the plaster wall, 12 or 15 feet away from the officials whose voices
were further muted by a plexiglass barrier. When Mr. Scary yelled "RMPRHS
RNRFF MNRFFF!!" he didn't get a lot of takers. So more people crept forward, crowded into the small space in front of the counters, trying to hear the

announcement of the names. Mind you, they were too petrified to approach the windows, but unless you were directly in front of the doorway, you couldn't hear anything but your own crazed heartbeat.

"MPHFHPH MPPFFHH!!" he shouted, and a lone victim with bionic hearing slowly advanced toward Sportello Numero Tre.

Signore Scary barked at every document, and then yelled some more. The applicant was ordered to stand against the doorway, against an attached yardstick. Maybe Signore Scary was trying to decide if the applicant was as tall as he claimed on his passport, or maybe he was measuring aorta height for the firing squad. I couldn't tell.

More people crowded in, apparently at random. Some approached the counters and were served by the first two officials, some dropped their letters onto the counter at the Filing Department at Sportello Numero Four, but after a few minutes Mr. Scary waved them off, and then shouted, "Get outside! Wait outside! I said it 50 times!!"

Humble myself? I was about to wet myself. My documents were efficiently filed in Sportello Numero Four, and I had no idea when I would be called back; for all I knew, they were calling people who had been standing there for days. I was hoping that I wouldn't be called by Signore Scary, because I would have cracked way before the waterboarding started. But I also had a smirk on my face that would have gotten me thrown out of an eighth-grade assembly. In this room, I could get a one-way ticket to a tour of the Catacombs.

I have a horrible time with authority. I quit the Camp Fire Girls because I can't do anything in unison, like recite a creed and wear a uniform. But overbearing authority makes me laugh. In a room full of petrified people and a guy who thinks he's Joseph Stalin, I giggled.

My chances of surviving a review of my papers were dicey. If Sportello Uno called me, he could assure me in English that the torture methods they planned to use at the deportation facility had been personally approved by Dick Cheney. If I were called by Numero Due, his eyes were a distraction from my fate. But if Numero Tre called me, I was doomed.

Sportello Numero Due, the only official directly in front of the doorway, so of course the only one who used a microphone, enunciated clearly into the mic. And thankfully, he called my name. I stepped forward. He was so attractive that I didn't want to spoil it for all of us by showing him my photo. He wanted my passport. *Nessun problema*—no problem. He wanted my phone number—now we're getting somewhere. Because I was too afraid to speak, I showed him that it was written on the back of my phone. And then he asked about our kids.

So that was it, they were going to take the children. Not having seen my impressive stretch marks, Sportello Due didn't believe we had reproduced. "Where are the children?" he asked.

"At school," I answered. This seemed to please him. The muscles of his face, which seemed as tight as a ball of elastics, loosened slightly. Oh, he *is* human!

"You need to bring photos of the children." Of course I knew that, because it was written in the application. Or in the letter from the Questura. Okay, no, it wasn't. Andy approached the counter, showed Numero Due his letter.

"Do I need photos of the children, too?"

"Yes. Bring them to me on Wednesday. At 8:30." He took out a form, wrote the date and time of our next appointment, and added: "Bring photo of son." I helpfully pointed out that we also have a daughter, and he actually smiled. A smile from the Questura is a rare and wonderful thing.

I looked back behind us, at the crowd in the doorway. There was a mass of humanity, fanned out, hoping to catch a clue as to what to do, all terrified. These are the crowds that climb onto trains because someone tells them to do so. And these were the people who told Andy and me to go to the front, to drop off our letter. Maybe they had been standing there since the electronic number board had stopped working, in 1983. I got a smile from the Questura. And an invitation to do it all again on Wednesday.

We're outta here, Toto.

Chapter 20
Doctor Who?

After several delicious and terrifying months in Italy, we had made no progress on obtaining a Permesso, and had many unanswered questions, including how to obtain medical care. In Italy there aren't many private doctors, because Italians have established a system of—no, don't say it—socialized medicine.[13] There are doctors, hospitals, clinics—a whole free medical system—but we needed permission from the government to use them. Did our visa allow us to access Italian health care? If not, how could I contact an Italian doctor who took private insurance?

In our first burst of settling-in activity, Giovanna took us to an office that provided access to the medical system for Italians and other people living in Italy. Giovanna thought that since were living there for a year, we were entitled to access—*don't say it*—socialized medicine. So she took us to ASL, the office that processed those permits.

It was a typical government office: a long line of people holding numbers for no apparent reason. But Giovanna jumped the line, popped into a doorway, and soon she was speaking in rapid Italian with government officials about our situation. The officials scrutinized our documents and concluded that Andy and I couldn't use the health system because he was being paid by an American university, not an Italian one.

What about the children? There was a heated conversation in Italian, and the gist of it was that, to keep the children, we'd have to go to the American Embassy in Florence. Apparently, there are consequences for failing to take a number at an Italian government office.

---

13   Dale, my best friend in college, had a very conservative brother, "Myron the surgeon." In the thick of a family argument, Dale's brother spat out: "Go ahead SAY IT—socialized medicine!!" which was apparently Myron's idea of being the guest of honor at a flaying festival. It's been 40 years, and I can't hear "socialized medicine" without laughing.

Well, that was a new one. We were not only *not* entitled to medical care, but we also weren't going to be able to keep the children, unless we went to Florence. Not that I'm averse to a trip to Florence, but this time, I was willing to call the Italians' bluff. These particular children were high maintenance, and I knew that even if the Italian government took them, they wouldn't keep them for very long. So a trip to Florence was out, at least until the weather warmed up enough to stand in line to see the statue of David. Maybe seeing David would put me in the mood to ask for the kids back.

We dodged the Florence visit, and no one came for the kids. But one day, Alex got sick. He stopped eating, which hadn't happened for two consecutive minutes since he had turned 11. That was a worry. He looked gelatinous and slumpish, which is fine for a squid, but not for a kid who never stopped knocking various body parts into the furniture. He wasn't sick enough to take to the ER, but he could have qualified for a strep test. He'd never had strep, but Annalise could have died from a virus that mutated into a life-threatening illness, so I never think, "It's just a virus." I think, "Thank God I have insurance." In Italy, I thought, "Thank God for socialized medicine," but I was raised by Republicans, so that would be wrong.

I asked friends in Modena if they knew a doctor who spoke English, and thought I found one. But he didn't speak the kind of English that would let us know whether Alex had strep or required a knee replacement. And the doctor's office was open only from 10:00 a.m. to 10:07 a.m. on Tuesday, maybe Wednesday. But definitely not Thursday, or Monday through Friday. Either Italy had a particularly healthy population so that doctors were completely unnecessary, or Italians got sick only in increments of seven minutes or less.

So I turned to the American Embassy, in Florence, that beacon of hope for Americans abroad, staffed with public servants paid for by my tax dollars. In the movies, when the going gets tough, the tough go to the Embassy. All I had to do was to reach the gates; once I was on hallowed ground, brave Embassarians would sweep me through the doors under a slurry of gunfire, graciously serving tea with one hand while smothering firebombs with the other. Those people were poised to finesse every catastrophe. They could solve any problem that could befall any American, especially if the American were Angelina Jolie.

Surely, they could tell me how to find a doctor in Italy?

So I emailed the embassy. I laced the subject line with a reference to a sick child, hoping to play on their sympathy, but it took over two weeks to get a response. Apparently, the Embassy will help only those who can survive the wait for assistance. Better hang out in front of the gates, or ask them to pencil you in about two, three weeks before you anticipate a crisis. But I'll bet Angelina Jolie gets in without an appointment.

My email asked whether Andy's sabbatical ("study") visa entitled us to use the Italian medical system for medical care for our kids. This is their actual response:

RE: Medical Coverage for Minors Under Parents' Study Visa–Sick Child
From: "Florence, USCitizens"

Thank you for your inquiry.

Apologies for not replying sooner.

As far as we are aware you need to pay an extra fee at the Italian post office in order to apply for the Italian medical insurance through ASL, although you should contact your local USL/ASL office for more information.

Regards, American Citizen Services US Consulate General Florence

They attached a list of doctors who spoke English, in their "consular district." Their consular district included Estonia and the International Space Station, but nothing remotely close to Modena. And the reference to the post office was clearly an effort to push me over the edge.

I replied:

Thank you for your response, but I would appreciate some clarification. Do you live in Italy? The suggestion that one can waltz into an Italian post office, pay an extra fee, and actually leave with a resolution of a problem involving medical documentation is sheer madness. I'm lucky if I can buy stamps.

The Embassy never responded. They were too busy getting their free flu shots at a clinic in their consular district in Tasmania, or they were helping Angelina Jolie resolve a problem regarding a FedEx. I considered mailing them a box of squid.

Chapter 21
Rescue Me

My Italian key ring looked like a prop from *The Da Vinci Code*. While I was still in a jet-lagged stupor, our landlord, Raimondo, gave me seven keys, the use of which he explained in rapid Italian, which means not at all. Each key was shaped like it was made by a blacksmith with a personality disorder, and each door had several sets of keyholes, some of which dated to the building's post-war construction, and some to the Middle Ages.

There were 7 keys and 600 potential keyholes. We had a key to open the door to the street, another for the cellar storage unit, one for the mailbox, and another to escape from the enclosed patio (there didn't seem to be a key to *enter* the patio, which made me wonder whether I wanted to go there at all). And there was the key to the door to the roof, that led to the view of Fabio's balcony, and Fabio. Let's all go back and read about Fabio again.

Sigh.

To open the apartment door, which was made of iron-hard oak, required two keys, which had to be turned in opposite directions, 400 times each. No wonder Romeo had to climb up the shrubbery to reach Juliet—she wouldn't have had time to let him in through an Italian door before their parents killed each other or they started dating other people.

But one day, our keys didn't work, which required the glorious intervention of Italian firefighters.

Here's what happened:

On a dreary Sunday after a snowy Saturday, two days of quality time in our cramped apartment left us festering like six-month-old sushi[14], so we escaped

---

14   I know what living with six-month-old festering sushi is like, because Alex left a package of that exact thing under his bed, for six months. For six months I maniacally scrubbed the apartment floors, trying to eradicate that smell, because WHO WOULD THINK THAT SMELL WAS ROTTING FISH? We didn't find the sushi until we were packing to leave for the US. That is why I constantly have this look on my face. No really, that is *why*.

to a nearby park. The park was just a stroll away, which in Italy means you pass gelato stands, excellent shoes, and 1,000 years of history.

Let loose onto gravel paths and muddy fields, the kids burned off some of the manic energy they had been using to annoy me. I took a walk, Andy got in a run, and we all met up to read the park information sign. The park was dedicated to the memory of Modena Resistance fighters—*i partigiani*—who hid in these fields while fighting Italian Fascists and Nazis at the end of WWII.

We wandered, we read, we learned, until the offspring were tired enough to be safely let back into captivity.

We climbed the seven flights up to our apartment. The building had an elevator, but "Let's take the stairs!" was another ploy to wear out the kids. Besides, the elevator was about 200 years old and the size of an envelope. If I was fated to be trapped and die in something, I preferred it to be bigger than the decorative urn for my crematory ashes.

Happy to be home after a walk, a run, and seven flights of stairs, Andy plunged his keys into the locks, but the door wouldn't open. A million tries, the door stayed shut. Raimondo heard us on the landing and tried his keys. Andy's keys. His keys. We had nowhere else to go—it was Sunday, and in Italy, everything was closed, even the big malls. Desperate to get us off his landing, Raimondo called a locksmith, and invited me and the kids into his apartment to wait while he and Andy pretended that the hundredth time was the charm.

The locksmith arrived in 20 minutes, with a reassuring smile. Forty-five minutes later, his smile sagged, and Raimondo looked alarmed. The apartment doors in that building were at least three inches of solid, aged oak. Italian crime dramas must never show a grim-faced detective busting down a door, because the cop's bones would be shattered like confetti.

Raimondo sent us back into his apartment, but that was a poor tactical move on his part. Once we were in his apartment, he'd either have to send us back onto the landing or get us back into our apartment. Raimondo's options were not good. He could put us up for the night and break down the door in the morning, or break down the door tonight. Raimondo was no fool—he was better off taking his losses immediately. We couldn't even go to a hotel: when Andy goes running, he leaves his wallet at home. I had no more money than… okay, due to the debacle involving my missing debit card, everyone in the whole world had better access to money than I did.

To lighten the mood, I asked Raimondo about the Italian Resistance, Fascism, and the Nazi occupation of Modena. (Melanie told me later that bringing up the war to an Italian is a *faux pas* only slightly less offensive than having milk in coffee after 10 a.m.). As a guest, I left a lot to be desired. So, Raimondo opted for a desperate and potentially expensive solution: he called the fire department. For Raimondo, calling the fire department summoned the specter of splintering wood and shattering glass, but that was preferable to listening to me discussing a national tragedy in fractured Italian.

Twenty minutes later, the *vigili del fuoco* arrived. In a ladder truck! I was now five years old, and there was a ladder truck outside our building!! Things were looking up, and those things included fabulous Italian firefighters.

The firefighters piled into the elevator—they were braver than I thought. They tried Andy's keys. They tried Raimondo's keys. They slipped a plastic thing between the jamb and the door. Nothing. They inserted a sinister-looking metal thing into the jamb. I winced for Raimondo.

How many firefighters does it take to open an Italian door? More than we had. And they couldn't get a battering ram up in that elevator. I think this cheered up Raimondo, as much as a landlord can be cheered up when there are four Americans and six firefighters on his landing.

There was no way to open the door from the outside. And then dawned the delightful possibility: would they have to use their fancy ladder? Just for us? How cool is that? [I tried to readjust my expression to a concerned grownup face but gave up and went onto Raimondo's balcony to giggle maniacally at the flashing lights spilling from the ladder truck and playing over the walls of adjacent buildings.]

The firefighters valiantly entered the bucket and ascended through spiny trees, up and up… seven stories. Neighbors gathered on their balconies; onlookers clustered across the street. "It's the Americans!" they must have thought. "They're too stupid for keys!!" I hoped they weren't recollecting that in WWII

Americans bombed Modena in order to liberate the city from the Nazis. And here we followed up with this. On a Sunday, no less.

The firefighters clambered over the railing onto the balcony—the balcony door was locked. Nooooo!! But the small balcony window that opened into the kitchen was unlocked. Yaaaaay! They squeezed through the window, streamed past the soup we left on the stove and the roast potatoes we left in the oven. THANK GOD I decided to shut everything off before we left, because I actually did think: "What if firefighters had to enter the building and the stove was on?" Sometimes, I am actually good at this "Don't Be an Idiot" thing.

The firefighters opened the door from the inside… and what was the problem? The door chain, that hung innocently beside the door jamb, got caught in the door as it swung shut. The harder we pushed, the more the metal of the chain embedded into the rock-solid wood. The only solution was the delightfully awesome Firefighters/Ladder Truck/Cool Bucket option.

Everyone was happy. The firefighters were happy; they demonstrated unparalleled courage in using the elevator, and they made everybody jealous by going up so high in their cool bucket. We were happy because we were back in the apartment. And Raimondo was happy because nothing was broken in the rescue, and he didn't have to live with us for the remaining months of our lease and discuss the Resistance.

A great adventure involves cool hardware and no claims against insurance. That was a great adventure.

Chapter 22
The Kids Are Alright

The year we lived in Italy, Alex turned 13 and Annalise turned 7. Because they were so far apart in age, it was a challenge to find a school that would take them both. They didn't speak Italian, and in our pre-COVID-19 innocence we assumed that if we were all going to survive a year in Italy, home schooling wasn't an option.

Fortunately, we found an international school that accepted them both, and most of our money. The school was in Montale, a town with a single coffee bar that we reached on a meandering bus on a day as damp and chilly as the refrigerated freezer at Mario's. Our meeting was for 11 a.m., so we had time for coffee before meeting with Mrs. Stephens, the American school director. I ordered a latte. *"Una latte?"* asked the waiter, who was unimpressed with my Starbucks Italian.

"Si, una latte."

"Una laaaattte?" he asked again, then brought me a glass of milk. Sadly, my first cup of Italian coffee was lost in translation.

We walked about a mile to the school, on streets that buzzed with cars but had no sidewalks. To avoid traffic, we scraped against fences, many of which barely held in bored and frustrated dogs who hurled themselves against iron railings they could have easily jumped over, which added a tang of suspense to our terror. We finally reached the school's gate, and Mrs. Stephens was not there. Neither was anyone else.

Andy checked his phone messages. He had gotten the time wrong; our appointment was for 10 a.m., not 11. Andy, who prides himself on his flawless mastery of logistical details, had gotten the time wrong?? Unlike his logistically challenged family, "These Things Did Not Happen" to my spouse. He was mortified, and convinced that he was losing his mind, so of course he refused to talk to any of us for the rest of the day.

We retraced our steps, and because Andy was distraught at his error, we tried to keep our faces supportively neutral. When we got back to Modena, Andy disappeared up the steps of a medieval palazzo to mourn the loss of his faculties, while Alex, Annalise, and I crept along the side of the building and collapsed with laughter.

Friends asked how the kids liked school in Italy. They attended a private school that cost as much as a Maserati because the students were the offspring of people who *make* Maseratis, Ferraris, and oddly, shelf-stable packaging for liquids like milk and soup. As a perk to lure the best workers from all over the world, these companies provided free tuition for employees' children. Pavarotti's offspring also went there, which explained the wide halls and excellent cafeteria food. But now you know why a Ferrari costs so much: field trips to Florence and full-color yearbooks for every child.

Of course, we got our money's worth. There were constant updates on the kids' progress. Every week, Annalise's teacher, Ms. Sweeney, stunned us with the shocking news that Annalise could read. Out loud, even! Every Friday, Annalise's "Homework Diary" included a Post-it Note with the same breathless announcement. "Annalise read *The Boy Who Fell in the Well and Nearly Died* clearly and with expression!!" Annalise was seven years old and had been reading for four years. Ms. Sweeney's weekly discovery of Annalise's reading ability was *Ground Hog Day*-esque. How many times did Annie Sullivan announce that little Helen learned the sign for water? You can milk that for only so long before parents want to know about long division. After 24 versions of the same update, my enthusiasm for this news started to flag. If Ms. Sweeney continued to be startled that Annalise could read, to avoid unnecessary excitement, I declined to mention that she had also graduated to finger food.

While I wasn't shocked that Annalise could read, I *was* surprised at the content of the books offered to second graders. One of the first books Annalise took out of the school library was about Paddington, the adorable British bear rescued from a train station. But in the school's version, Paddington was kidnapped and held for ransom by a thuggish gang of badgers. Although I tried to maintain my parenting edge, I wasn't expecting illustrations of Paddington hog-tied and threatened by his abductors. In another book, a young prince was kidnapped by his evil uncle who threw the boy in jail, took all his money, and extorted cash from the rest of the villagers until peace was restored through several pages of violence involving paw-to-paw combat and spears that glinted in sun *and* moonlight. Yikes. Then there was a chipper read about tots caught in a devastating flood that destroyed their furniture and almost killed them, and another about the strafing of London, with an informative aside on the necessary discomfort of wearing gas masks.

I'm no fan of fairy tales; in all the "princess is saved by a kiss" books, I tacked on an epilogue that the prince was a whiz with a toilet brush, and the day after the wedding, the princess started medical school. I didn't *do* fluff. But Paddington's struggle with rope burns and post-traumatic stress disorder was a bit much for second graders. The library books were British. If this is what kids in England grow up reading, I can see where Winston Churchill got his moxie; apparently Neville Chamberlain skipped second grade.

Although classes were taught in English, Annalise and Alex both studied Italian for four and a half hours a week. At least once a week, Annalise came home with a bulging blue notebook: Italian homework. Italian homework consisted of worksheets that helped the kids practice Italian vocabulary. The children were supposed to write each vocabulary word next to the picture provided. However, the illustrations were indecipherable scribbles. What Italian word was meant by that hairy looking ball of clay? Or that hook-ish item crooked at an odd angle? I couldn't fake the perky "Oh honey, *you* know what *that* is" essential to noncommittal homework assistance.

We knew that Annalise's Italian teacher patiently introduced each new vocabulary term and reinforced each day's lesson by reproducing the words all over the classroom: she wrote them on the board, wove them into the rug, carved them into the marble of the school room floor. Ms. Isabella was not keeping those words a secret from the children. But *I* had no idea what the little symbols meant. And Annalise swore that she was held captive in a cave, like Paddington, while those words were discussed in class.

To ratchet up the agony, each week the vocabulary words involved a different cluster of letters. For example, Annalise was supposed to identify words with the letters "gna" or "gno" at the end, or even worse, in the middle. Sure, you say, "I know a word with 'gna' at the end, lasagna!!" Just maybe, if the little sketch looked like a pasta dish instead of an infected sponge, I could have filled in that blank, Mister Smarmy. But the intrepid Ms. Isabella required not one, but 12 words which end in "gna." And the accompanying illustrations mystified me: what's an Italian word that looks like a boulder partially submerged by the sea that has "qua" in the middle? There is no dictionary that allows you to find a word using that information. So, when the blank lines beckoned, Annalise took the Fifth, and Andy and I were left to figure it out for ourselves. At approximately $40 per vacant line, we couldn't afford to let any bit of knowledge get past us.

Just when we thought we'd put the child up for adoption over the worksheet fiasco, Ms. Isabella upped the ante: she started asking the kids to write "little stories" based on those well-loved vocabulary words. "Fine," you say (you're starting to develop quite an attitude there, Buster). "How hard could that be?" But the story had to include those 12 terms, and no others.

The vocabulary lists included only nouns, not verbs. How do you write a story using only nouns? Don't the nouns have to *do* something to constitute a story? For example, in *War and Peace*, a lot of people engaged in warlike activities, and then in peaceful ones. Action words, people, they're out there. But Annalise claimed total innocence on the subject of verbs, and there were no verbs on the vocab lists. And although on the playground Annalise slung vowels like she was born in Rome, when faced with the Bulging Blue Notebook she claimed complete ignorance of conjugation. There are a million different verb endings in Italian based on the number, gender, and shoe size of the noun that goes with them. There's a reason they call them verb *tenses*. So Andy, who is a lunatic, allowed her to write her story in English, and then he translated it for her.

Annalise, freed from the onerous task of learning Italian, spun the list of words into a novel-length flight of fancy. Andy translated her story into Italian, but stoically provided a Reader's Digest version in one terse paragraph. Annalise, upon learning that her Byronic prose had been stripped to the emotive flair of a bus schedule, seethed at the injustice of being edited by a hack. Then the yelling started. The study of languages brought us all closer—to homicide.

The Cat, aka Annalise, was also disturbed by the school's snack policy. The kids were required to go outside every day, and they had to eat outside. She didn't want yogurt for a snack. "It's cold outside, and I have to stand in the cold damp terrain and eat cold yoghurt." We tried pistachio nuts, but pistachios violated the school policy against nuts. We considered other options: crackers, cheese, Clementines? No, no, and there was a girl in her class named Clementine. "Maybe I will eat her instead," the Cat said darkly. Pending a policy change, snacks were out.

When the kids weren't at school, they were travelling. To London, Paris, Rome, even Legoland Denmark. They saw so much: the Anne Frank House. The Louvre. Westminster Abbey. Notre Dame on Easter Sunday. Venice at sunset. Normandy in the 65th anniversary of the D-Day Invasion. Fifty cities in a year.

They got an insider's view of European history, and an outsider's view of America. But they missed a few days of school along the way. If they were going to be absent, we were required to request permission from their teachers, and we were informed that permission for them to leave might not be granted.

Now we were getting somewhere. We would have been fine if the kids couldn't miss class!! While Andy and I headed to Paris, Annalise could hang out with Ms. Isabella, and they could get cracking on some verbs, including, "Do your homework" and "Go to sleep." And Ms. Sweeney, who never tired of hearing Annalise learn to read, could surprise herself with Post-it updates the whole time we were away. Alex had so far escaped the gritty underworld of the second-grade library, but camping out there could have been his finest hour, and it's never too late to learn about the perils of poison gas.

Chapter 23
Imagine

As parents do, we made friends with the parents of our kids' school friends. While the kids hung out, we had a cappuccino in the park with Elena and Edward, whose son Alexander went to school with Alex and Annalise. Talking to them was fascinating. They grew up in a Communist country behind an Iron Curtain that has rusted and fallen away. What was that like? Elena laughed. "The government was not Communist. There were a few ruling families with all of the power. The children and grandchildren of those people were sent to good schools. Now the children and grandchildren of those same people are in charge of the government. There is no difference."

I hear the sound of friends' voices long after the conversation, and my thoughts take on that accent. In my head, Elena's voice is deep and low and lovely.

Our kids went to school with 100 children from 17 different countries. Only four kids, including our own, were American. The school attracts families from all over the world because the parents are contractors for international companies like Ferrari and Maserati. Contracts lasted from one to five years; when they ended, families moved to a different country, or to a different part of the world. Our American friends thought we were crazy to spend a whole year away from home, and the contract families thought we were crazy to stay for only a year.

I had only a year, and there was so much to learn. So many stories. Before living in Italy, Elena, Edward, and Alexander lived in Shanghai, for four years. "Can you imagine?" Elena asked, in her Italian apartment with the Chinese silk table runner. Over coffee, I tried. Alexander, born in Bulgaria, was enrolled in a Chinese school at the age of four, where he learned to speak Chinese and English. And now they lived in Italy, where he learned Italian, and he excelled at that too. Can you imagine?

In the park, Elena made a funny slip. Describing a friend that she met when her friend was in her 30s, Elena said, "She committed suicide. At 16."

I corrected her. "She *tried* to commit suicide." We laughed. But Elena speaks multiple languages—Bulgarian, Chinese, Italian, English, and some Russian; I can't remember them all. I corrected the grammar of a person who speaks so many languages I can't list them. We laughed, and I apologized that my Bulgarian and Chinese were a bit rusty.

I wanted to know what it was like for Elena growing up. She lived for a time in Siberia, a small girl with four huge dogs, wandering the wilds of Russia. Can you imagine? No, please tell me all about it. And thank you for learning English, or I'd never know.

Our kids had friends from all over the world. Alex's Canadian friend had lived in London, Switzerland, and Italy, and he was soon leaving for boarding school in Scotland. Annalise's closest friends were twin boys who were born in India but had lived in Seattle. Other kids were from Brazil, and Serbia, and Spain. Annalise's teacher, who was British, spent four years in Poland. Alex's teachers were from Australia, England, Scotland, and Italy.

Not having a car was an inconvenience I felt most when there was a school function. Our apartment was a long bus ride and a harrowing walk from their school, and far from most other parents. To socialize, I had to ask for a ride. To get to a farewell lunch for a friend who was going back to America, I was offered a lift by a friend from England. We stopped for cappuccino and laughed about the endless battle with mosquitos and the frustrations of hitting a plateau in Italian.

Most of the women at the lunch had kids who attended the international school. I talked to an Italian mom, who had lived in London for ten years, about why she sent her Italian kids to a private school. I had the same conversation with her that I had with parents at our kids' school in the US: "It's not tough enough." "The teachers let the kids slide." "There's too much/not enough homework." But these parents compared the international school in Italy with ones their children had attended in France, and Singapore, and Sweden.

After lunch I got a ride home from Nicole, a gorgeous Italian. She had huge blue eyes in a flawless Mediterranean complexion, and she held herself with the languor of a feline, gracefully at ease. We talked about the book *Revolutionary Road,* a popular novel about a woman's rebellion against expected behavior for wives in the 1950s. Her perspective, as the wife of a very traditional Italian man, was fascinating. How much had changed for Italian wives? It depended on the marriage, she said.

In Italy I met people whose worldview was based on having lived all over the world. A mom at a school party was from Lebanon, but she spent four years in Tehran. What did she think about what was happening in Iran? "What should America do?" I asked.

"Stay back," she said. It took her a while to be comfortable enough to say she thought America was too close to Israel. She didn't want to offend us, and she certainly didn't hate us for our freedoms. Her perspective was shaped by living in the places Americans see only as maps on the news. It was fascinating to listen to people whose opinions were based not on viewing the world from a soapbox, but from buying soap in a market that may have been the site of a bombing. Can you imagine? I'll listen, and I'll remember that when bombs fall, the market is filled with good moms like this one.[15] She left the Middle East, but like many Americans, others stayed home. The news is about what happens to good people who stay.

Every conversation with a school parent was like a reflection from another facet of a mirrored ball. We were kindly offered a ride home from a school party by friends of Annalise's Indian friends. Most families didn't have cars big enough to carry an extra four people, so Andy and the kids went home with Elena and Edward, and I got a ride with friends of the twins. Their three-year-old son was irresistible in a Hawaiian shirt and carrying a toy electric guitar. This family arrived in Italy at the same time we did, in January, and we laughed at how we didn't expect it to be so cold.

"It was so hard" said the mom. "I couldn't figure out what to buy in the market, like how to buy bleach!" I had the same problem. Italian bleach doesn't look like Clorox. It's in a container like Soft Scrub, and it's called "Vanish" like our toilet cleaner. This beautiful woman, with blue eyes and a lovely sari, was wandering the market in the same confusion I was, looking for bleach. Can you imagine?

I asked the parents where they'd prefer to live. "If not Italy, then India, or an English-speaking country," the dad replied.

"The United States?" I asked.

"No, many Indians have the American Dream, but not us. We'd prefer the United Kingdom, or Singapore." Like my British pal, the Indian mom was frustrated with Italian. "I learned French and German well. But Italian has been difficult." I ask what other languages she spoke; she already knew her

---

15   In America, we don't worry about bombs hitting the market, we worry about active shooters in the market. Same carnage, different weapon.

native Indian language, and Hindi, and English, before she tackled French and German. Italian was her sixth language. "No wonder Italian is hard. Your brain cells are full!" We laughed, but I realized that "English Only" keeps Americans from discovering new, and old worlds.

What would I miss about Italy? The world.

Chapter 24
Tea and Sympathy

While the kids were in school, Andy was teaching, and I was averse to getting wet and couldn't spend any money, I spent a lot of time alone in the apartment, which made me write silly stories like this one. I hope it makes you laugh, too:

It's another cold and rainy day in Modena. Well, since it's rainy, I don't know whether it's cold; it's not like I need to know, and I like to mind my own business when I can.

Besides, I got an email from a friend in Denver with news about a sudden onset of painful shoulder-itis. Carolyn woke up with a hurt shoulder; I suspect stress. With rain ensuring that I don't have to learn anything more about the quirks of living in Italy until it stops, I can concentrate on sending a cheery and concerned response.

It's so amazing to answer an email and NOT HAVE TO DO ANYTHING ELSE!! In the States, I was maniacally busy. I was simultaneously practicing law, teaching it, preparing to abandon various ships, and living with people who inexplicably expected clean clothes and meals. So I am okey dokey with a little downtime.

Yet even now I am multi-tasking: I am typing while drinking tea and listening to James Taylor videos on YouTube. A cup of tea, a little email, some music, life is good.

So let's fire up a video; what's a good sore shoulder song to get us started? We'll go with "You've Got a Friend."

Hi Carolyn! I'm so sorry about your shoulder! How did it happen? How do you wake up with a sore shoulder? Is it tension? Because I can TOTALLY relate…

Okay, no I can't. But I needed to be empathetic, here. If it weren't for the yoga, and not having to work, and being in Italy, I'd be tense, too. So what do I say about that? When it's already time to pick a new video?

My email/listen-to-music plan had a fatal flaw. Did you ever notice how brief James Taylor songs are? They are so short that by the time you pick a video and get back to your email, the song is already over.[16] I think this is a problem with James Taylor that no one has discovered before. "James Taylor, he's so great, and he just gets better with age." Yada yada yada.

But doesn't anyone notice that his songs are only about three words long, and it takes no time at all to sing them?

*Why do **I** have to do all the hard work thinking of these things? Can't someone else do some of the heavy lifting? God, it's exhausting, and now I need a fresh cup of tea, and that doesn't get made by itself. I'm starting to get a little crick in my neck.*

Back to Carolyn's email. Where was I? Something about tension. I'll tell you about tension, pal. I'm listening to James Taylor and Carly Simon sing "You Can Close Your Eyes." YouTube tells me that video clocks in at just over two minutes. They'll belt it out for less time than it takes to boil water, and then I have to choose something else. A Carly Simon's solo is no better: "Blackbird," 2:36 – two minutes, 36 seconds. If I switch species, and go with both of them singing "Mockingbird," it's good for only 3:45.

*All these people **do** is sing. They're not doing anything hard, like drinking tea and hanging out in Italy. Can't they keep at it for longer than it takes to prepare a hot drink? Obviously, this slothfulness has led to the downfall of communication.*

While the rest of you are out there, in the rain, making money, I have discovered something scary: the whole texting thing, the "i cnt typ wth vwls" malarkey, is James Taylor's fault. His lack of effort has left us standing in line at Target typing seventeen letters on a tiny screen, and the utter annihilation of classical literature.

Why? Great books involve a lot of words on a lot of pages, and clearly, with this texting stuff, that's over. Young pups are ditching vowels and pitching punctuation, and we're all riding an emoticon straight to hell.

: (

But how is the demise of literature James Taylor's fault? James Taylor has a grip on the Boomer psyche that is positively anacondal. While today's whippersnappers were in utero, their parents listened to super-short songs like Sweet Baby James (2:06) and played them through-out their tots' formative years. Short James Taylor songs quite possibly predisposed children to expect only miniscule bursts of information, which inevitably, and tragically, led to texting.

---

16   This was before I figured out how to stream YouTube videos. But even now I defy YouTube algorithms, because they're not the Boss of me.

i m sd.

If people won't write out an entire sentence, why would they read a book, especially a long one? Who needs to read War and Peace, when you can say it all in three consonants and a vowel? Here is War and Peace in text:

i m sd. :).

Russian novels are so depressing, even peace time was a downer. If Tolstoy were texting "Wr n Ps" today, he could have described the war and the peace of 1812 without even tacking on the cheery emoticon at the end:

i m sd.

*So what is the point of sending Carolyn some lame email about the potential causes of her injury? Here's all that **ever** needs to be said: i m sd.*

*Now you've done it. I'm too depressed for tea. Carolyn is wounded, communication is dead, and you're expecting Florence Nightingale. Does anyone care how **I** feel?*

I need to find another YouTube video, and the stress is starting to lock up my shoulder. : [

Chapter 25
Deliverance

After three months of calls and emails to FedEx and my bank, waiting in the apartment for a buzzer that never rang, I happened to be outside our building, waiting for the kids to get off their bus, when I heard an odd sound: "Go-etz? Go-etz?" In the parking lot across the traffic circle from our building, and coincidentally within hearing distance of my kids' bus stop, a FedEx delivery driver was standing outside his truck, calling into the air, not to anyone in particular. But because there quite possibly is a God, I heard him anyway. He was holding an envelope like it was as infected as the sponge representing lasagna in Annalise's Italian worksheet. I practically flew the hundred feet to his truck.

"I.AM. GO-ETZ."

I signed. I had a bank card. Could you hear angels singing? That might have been the sound of the ATM keys as I pressed my account numbers. And I could finally go shopping.

Chapter 26
Finding the Street Market – All Was Not Lost, but I Was

I knew for months that every Monday in Modena, there was an open-air market that cruelly I couldn't find. The first several times I gave it a go, I was too bewildered by the tiny winding streets to trust that I'd ever get out again. Andy said I could get there on the bus, but I have always been suspicious of the entire "this bus has a specific route and stops only at these stops" theory. I have the same problem with trains and subways.

I may be alone in this, but I don't believe that subway trains *always* go where the map says they go. For example, in London the subway is called the Underground. Since the trains are buried, it's difficult for them to escape and go somewhere other than the holes that have been dug for them, but it *could* happen. There are multiple lines, and theoretically, the London Circle Line stops only at the places designated on the map on the wall of the subway train. You can tell that the train authorities take this route nonsense seriously because the route map is permanently painted onto the enamel wall of the subway car, and the different routes are assigned different colors, like yellow, green, and blue. Or that's what they *want* you to think.

Sure, that's what the map says, but every subway train has a driver, whose only job is to steer the train around the little track all day. How do *you* know how the driver is feeling about that? I leave open the possibility that a London Underground driver could decide that if he takes one more run through the Yellow Line stops of Binghampton on Pickle, Pinkington on Poppinshire, and Chopmutton on Rye, he's going to lose it completely. How can you spend day after day, underground, stopping at places that make you giggle if you say them out loud?

I personally balk at routine, so I imagine that the driver could tire of the monotony and spontaneously switch to a different track, from, say, the Yellow to the Blue Line. Or maybe he could dodge and weave and combine the Yellow and Blue lines into a very confusing Green Line. Or he could mix several routes, which would result in an unpredictable and unattractive Grayish Brown Line. It could happen, and *then* where would you be? You would have no idea, because you put your faith in an enameled map. *I'm* not that gullible.

Perhaps the difficulty at the heart of our marriage is that Andy studies transportation logistics and planning. Transportation experts have a confidence in train propaganda that is positively Orwellian. "Of *course* this train stops in Modena—that's what it says on the train schedule. And on the map. And on the board in the station. *And* on the electronic screen beside the track." Talk about drinking the Kool-Aid. So Andy studies the maps and the timetables and buys tickets, and we end up where we intended. Or maybe he's just pretending that's where he intended us to go; he knows I won't check.

Because I don't believe in all this planning. If the train people were so good at planning, why do you always have to walk downstairs to get to the track, and then back up again on the other side? If transportation experts were all that good at thinking ahead, they'd know that I packed way too much in my suitcase to lug it up and down 500 steps, each way.

So, I don't believe in the whole "you can't get lost because they're experts and they tell you where the train stops" thing. Besides, I subscribe to the Willie Wonka Theory of Transportation Management: if you push a button on the elevator, it could go up, down, sideways, diagonally, or straight through the roof. How do I *know* that subway trains can't poke new tunnels if the driver is bored with the old ones? *I* do not rely on the sanity of strangers holding steering wheels. Where do you think the phrase "driving me crazy" came from?

Funny, Andy uses it a lot.

So even in little Modena, I wasn't falling for the "it's easier to take the bus" theory. A bus driver has a lot more leeway than a subway driver. Bus drivers can do wheelies, donuts, and blow this town and head for Crespellano. Throughout this book, I may have made certain unkind remarks about Crespellanians failing to forward the FedEx package containing my replacement debit card. A one-way ticket to Crespellano would have been disastrous; obviously, blindly trusting a bus driver could have ended badly for me.

But I did have a Plan B, for those transportation logistics planners who believe in that kind of thing. If I got lost on foot, I always had the option of collapsing on the sidewalk, tucking myself into the fetal position, and sobbing quietly until I figured out what to do. So walking, rather than taking a bus to the market, was my best option.

And besides, walking is the whole point of Italy. When you walk, you glide past sidewalk cafes where deep and rich Italian syllables bubble up like *acqua minerale* from a shaded spring. Look up and there are dark eyes, mahogany curls, and the plane of a cheek that should be carved in marble and resting in the afternoon sun of a museum. Look down and there are a multitude of shoes, of soft and radiant leather, and as cleverly functional as a well-designed building,

And everywhere, there is black.. Black cashmere, wool, silk. Italian black is not listless and sad, it's precise, definitive, intriguing. The shade is so deep that it crisply excludes itself from everything around it. Here is the sharp blue sky, here is the gray speckled sidewalk, and here is the black coat that moves so elegantly past every lesser thing. In every part of my life I crave color, but on the streets of Modena, I luxuriated in black.

Through mud-specked bus windows, black looked like black everywhere else. So, I walked to the market. And with every step, I arrived at my destination.

Chapter 27
Agoraphobia Means "I Miss TJ Maxx"

I packed only enough clothes for about 20 minutes in Italy, and running up and down seven flights of stairs to dispose of tea bags, and having to walk even to obtain drinking water meant I lost weight, and, okay, because… Italy, I needed to buy clothes.

Although I steadfastly maintained my terror of getting lost, I was determined to find Modena's open-air market, which was open from 9 a.m. to 2 p.m. I never saw the opening of the market, because I never got out of the house before the crack of noon. It's not *just* that I was lazy and spending way too much time on Facebook. When I left the apartment, stuff happened, like getting locked out and having to be let into our apartment by firefighters in a ladder truck. Or having to fight the Italian government just to buy stamps. It was intimidating, I tell you.

I desperately needed to buy jeans, but in Modena shops, I felt like a slacker. First, there were the prices. The jeans in the shop on the way to the supermarket cost $225 euros. The price tag was attached to only one leg of the pants, but I hoped that the price covered both of them. And those insanely expensive jeans were already as faded and ripped as the ones I was trying to replace. The logic of paying *more* for tattered clothing escapes me. I preferred to invest in something crisp and classic that could enhance my appearance, like a tarp.

Even the process of buying jeans in a store was scary. Melanie, who knows everything, told me that when you buy clothes in an Italian shop, you do not browse, have a looksee, touch the merch. Italian clothing sizes are consistent, so you walk in, tell the clerk your size, and she gets it for you. The purchase is already complete before you touch the pants.

That would not work for me. Like my husband Andy (who is 6'4"), I'm not a size found in nature. I'm petite and short-waisted but have long legs, so I must try things on. In the US I often try on ten pairs of jeans before I find one that fits. And it's not like clothing manufacturers make any effort to meet my needs: "Okay, designers. Cut something to fit a person who's freakishly short with long legs but no waist. And she's been hitting the Cheetos pretty hard lately, so let them out a little."

I don't bond seamlessly with clothing; I like to know I'll respect us both in the morning. I try something on, wait a minute, and try it on again to see if I've lost any weight in between. At TJ Maxx I don't wear out my welcome, and no one has a fit.

But not in Italy. My friend Valerie described a harrowing visit to an Italian clothing store: she looked around, and when she attempted to compliment the clerk on the merchandise, the clerk threw her out, shouting something Valerie didn't understand. If you're tossed out on your keister for browsing, what happens to people who want to check for weight loss?

But then a surly clump of *Penne all'Arrabbiata* left a smear on my best jeans; I couldn't keep walking around town hunched to the right with my palm over the stain. Rather than swan dive directly into the churning rapids of a clothing shop, I planned to dog-paddle my way into the stream of commerce, through the open-air market.

The market was set up in a giant ring around a park just outside of the oldest part of Modena. One minute I was on a Modena street with all the gravitas of a museum, and the next I was sucked into the swirling vortex of the Yard Sale from Hell. There were hundreds of stalls selling clothing, housewares, shoes. The stalls were metal frames topped with canvas, with merchandise swaying from the rafters. Under the tents, there were tables loaded with merchandise, either neatly stacked or heaped in a frenzy of fabrics.

It was overwhelming. Crouched near the entrance was a heavy metal riot of espresso pots, cooking pans, cheap vegetable peelers. The shiny surfaces threw off slivers of sunlight as sharp as knives. Shoe sellers constructed fortresses of boxes topped with suede boots, sneakers, and stilettos so spiked they threatened to pierce the box lids. The color for that fashion season was purple, so there were racks of drapey polyester blouses in purple and black, leather jackets and trench coats in plum. There were cascades of soft scarves in shades so radiant it looked like a rainbow had slipped gently to earth. And in a startling illustration of the Madonna/Whore principle, frothy white First Communion outfits shared rafter space with latex lingerie that would make a street walker blush.

I wasn't ready to buy jeans, so I started with shoes. Where were the real Italian shoes? Near the entrance there were countless stalls offering "amazing!" deals for one to five euros, but those were obviously badly made clodhoppers. There was another stall of elegant pumps, but those were designed for the grownup purposes of going to work or looking wealthy enough to not have to work. I was looking for summer flats, for meandering purposes only.

In a stall of summer shoes, I saw creamy flats for 12 euros, about 15 dollars. Those were either a good deal, or cheap knockoffs, I couldn't tell. I've been a vegetarian since I was 12, but I've always bought leather shoes, under the theory that no one stalks and kills Bessy for her hide. And with all this walking, I couldn't afford plastic shoes that shredded my feet.

In the United States, shoe materials are listed on the inside of each shoe, but not in Italy. I couldn't tell if the dreamy creamy flats were made of leather. But on the bottom of this shoe was a little clear sticker with a symbol for each shoe part: the upper, the lining, and the sole. There was a symbol for each of them; phew, that meant those shoes were leather.

The shoe seller approached. Of course, he was so adorable that of course I would buy these shoes, I might even pay extra for the box. Melanie gave me a size conversion chart, so my shoe size should be a 37.5. I asked for that size, and, his eyes never leaving my face, the shoe seller insisted, "Thirty-eight." No, 37.5, I said, but he didn't have that size in stock.

"Thirty-eight," he explained, and handed me the shoes.

I took them to the trying-on area, a folding chair deep within the fortress walls. He was right. They fit, and they were comfortable. I paid for the shoes, and noting that I'm a savvy shopper, he threw in the box for free.

I was *so* good at that market thing.

Except that at the next stall I noticed that the real leather shoes had an odd little symbol that looked like a cow hide. I checked my sticker again; my symbols were all diamonds, so I lost that round. But at least I didn't pay for the box.

Fortified by my sassy market savvy, I surveyed the clothing options. Some of the stalls had neatly folded shirts and sweaters, or jeans, but many had heaps of clothes all mixed together. The unstacked clothing was often just as good as the stacked stuff, but was often cheaper. At the lowest end of the scale, the cheapest clothes were sold for one or two euros a piece. The fabric looked good, but on closer inspection each piece had a defect, a small stain or a tiny tear in the cloth. I didn't have much time, and I wanted to focus on the good stuff.

How do you find the highest quality goods for the lowest prices in an Italian street market? After a couple of orbits of the stalls, I noticed that the good stuff was hidden behind a short but impermeable wall of *nonnas*, Italian grandmothers. Nonnas "know from" quality, know how to get the best deals, and they have time to sort through the mounds of clothing at the stalls with the best merchandise.[17].

Starting the next week, I planned to arrive earlier, follow them around, and hoped that I wasn't the same size as someone they knew. Oh, *right*, that was not an actual problem.

I found a stall with summer shirts. Perhaps out of gratitude for all the fabulous religious art, God gave Italian women large chests and small waists. I have neither, and there was no place to try on the shirts. I chose a size medium, hoping that the discrepancies in body parts would even out, especially since I have a huge appreciation for religious art. The seller assured me that if the shirts didn't fit, I could come back and exchange them the next Monday. And if the slot machine comes up three cherries, you can always ask for your money back. I was lucky if I could find the street market again, never mind one out of 800 vendors. But I kept the receipt, just in case.

In Italy, receipts are a serious business. By law, if you were stopped by the fiscal police within 50 meters of a shop and had merchandise but no receipt for it, both you and the shopkeeper could be fined. So even the flower seller in front of the train station was fastidious about receipts. He might sell you a handful of wilted petals, but you could be sure he'd give you a record of the purchase.

I bought two more shirts, also size medium. I was on a roll, and it was time to try my luck with jeans. There were jeans sellers everywhere, but there were few I wanted to buy. Most of them were encrusted with crystals, like barnacles from the hull of Vegas. I was too old and too cranky to draw attention to my aft, so I looked for something simple. In a stall run by a slender woman, I saw a pair of basic jeans.

---

17   Do you want the secret to buying fabulous Italian shoes at *nonna* prices? I know a guy: Luca Christian Cotti, aka "Il Prof." The boots he sold me were so comfortable I re-soled them three times, and when I mentioned him to my Italian friends, Annamaria proudly showed off a shoe with his logo. Luca's shoes are gorgeous, comfortable, and nonna-priced, and he'll ship to the US. His Insta is "La Boutique Del Prof," or he's on Facebook at "Veronica Mitrano."

According to Melanie's pants conversion chart, I needed size 32. I asked for a 32, and the seller's eyes narrowed in disgust. "Thirty-two is too big!" she said, although how she could tell that from glaring directly into my pupils, I had no idea. She held up a 28. I haven't had hips that narrow since I was seven. "No, they're too small. Thirty-two." I repeated, and she dug out a 32. It was huge; I'd get a closer fit with the tarp, so I asked for a 29. I held them up and…maybe they'd fit? I could always bring them back…I bought the jeans. Only when I was more than 50 meters away did I realize she hadn't given me a receipt. That made me feel like an outlaw with very narrow hips.

Although it was only 1:30, most of the clothing sellers were packing up, so I moved on to housewares. I needed clothespins, tape, and some thread. I found the clothespins and tape and was struck by the size of the sewing kits. In the US, cheap sewing kits offer a few needles and three inches of thread in black, white, red, and blue. In the market, for a euro, I got enough needles and thread to make several quilts. And the colors were dark and muted tones: black, grey, beige, brown, and olive. And greige, grolive, grown, and brolive. Apparently the "buy purple" craze hadn't hit the thread makers yet.

I beamed in triumph: I shopped the market! I had shirts, jeans, and shoes. I walked home, excited to try on my new clothes.

Sigh.

The jeans would fit if I cut out all of the eating I did when I was bored, and most of the eating I did to sustain life. Only two out of the five shirts fit. But the shoes were comfortable, and I could always make a quilt out of the stuff I couldn't take back. That must be why they sold me so much thread.

Greeks have a word, agoraphobia, that means "fear of the marketplace." In Italian, it must mean "I still need to buy pants."

Chapter 28
Fitting In

After six months, I was peering with horror down the slippery slope that would carry us back to our suburban lives in the United States. In some ways, going home would be a relief. In Italy, every transaction was a Rubik's cube—I got one side all lined up, the squares clicked into a coherent block of color, and I got a Surge O'Smarmy. But there was always a facet I didn't notice, and my brain had to twist and turn to make sense of another jumble of tiles. It was frustrating, but incredibly entertaining.

After six months I'd mastered the basic tasks: I could shop in the market, take a bus, even recharge my cellphone. But to buy clothing that fit, I had to get over my fear of trying stuff on.

Every time I played Size Roulette at the open-air market, I lost, so, like the Cowardly Lion, I finally got up "da noive" to ask the vendors if I could try on the pants. Some of the stalls had canvas booths that closed with Velcro, and some sellers offered the back of a van loaded with boxes. But none of the market "dressing rooms" had mirrors inside; to see yourself in the clothes, you had to subject yourself to the scrutiny of fabulous-looking Italians.

Unlike Italian women, I do not have breasts in bounteous abundance. Their rib cages are narrow, their waists are impossibly small, and their rears are fabulously not. Italian curves are as sinuous and dramatic as the winding roads used for car commercials. I'm built more like a sidewalk with uneven sections; a dress cut for an Italian was not cut out for me.

I like to receive bad news in private, and I didn't want to determine how I looked by the horrified faces of the lovely citizens of Modena.

I thought I'd hit on a clever solution: I held my cellphone at arms' length and took photos of myself in the clothes. The pictures were disturbing—my face was twisted from trying to find the right angle, and if that is how I look when I'm confused, I'm never going to ask another question.

While I was clicking away in a van, the vendor politely tapped on the door to ask what the *inferno* (hell) I was doing in her vehicle. She laughed and got me *uno specchio*—a mirror. Oh, why didn't I think of that?? Finally, I could buy clothes that I knew didn't fit.

Realizing that the sand in the hourglass was slipping to the half-empty mark, I pinned my Courage medal to my tattered fur, hit the Giallo Brick Road, and was thrilled with every bit of progress. We took books out of the library, I bought fruit at the neighborhood fruit stand, and I spent a delightful day in Bologna on my ogna.

My Italian was improving, but there was so much I couldn't say. We bought bikes, and while we were riding in the park, Annalise veered into the path of a man who was neatly piloting a prim upright while wearing an elegant suit and fabulous shoes. When he peered at me with cool indignation I apologized, but I would have liked to elaborate: "Please don't take it personally, I don't know why my daughter is trying to kill you." But Italian dictionaries don't cover "negligent bikicide," and "Open your book to page 20" was no more fitting than the buxom blouses in the street market.

Chapter 29
Piccolina

Although I was barely cut out to buy pants, buying an Italian bathing suit was even more of a stretch, and only when we planned a trip to Tenerife did I discover that I'd left my bathing suit back in Colorado. In one of my favorite memories of that year in Italy, Giovanna rescued me once again.

I was rabid to go shopping. I needed just a bathing suit, so of course I wouldn't buy anything else. Deep, low chuckle: I was living in Italy, I finally had a card that summoned euros, and I was breathing.

Giovanna kindly offered to take me to a shop that sold swimwear. Buying a bathing suit is about as much fun for women as circumcision is for men, but men must do that only once. In Italy, all the women are built like Sophia Loren, and I was built like Macaulay Culkin in his *Home Alone* years. Finding anything that fit me in that land of wasp waists and bounteous bosoms was as irrational as trying to find an Italian over the age of eight who was not smoking.

Giovanna drove to a shop that from the outside looked like a warehouse, but inside was a fountain of fabric delights. There were sheets, dresses, and suits in gelato shades and buttery textures that made me want to taste them all.

The bathing suits were pooled in three waist-high cardboard boxes. Giovanna and I pulled some out to try on, and the shop owner, her friend, came over to help.

"*Piccola...*" (small) she mused, staring at what was left of my chest after two children. She tossed aside some of our selections, looked at my chest again. "*Piccolina...*" (very small). More rummaging, more chest assessment. "*Si, si, piccolina...*"

ALRIGHT already. If she moved on to "*piccolissima*" I was going to scream.

She asked if I wanted a bikini. "No," I said, and I blamed that on the children. But really, together they weighed less than 15 pounds; my stretch marks were the result of never letting my jaws rest for the duration of either pregnancy. It was fun while it lasted, but you shouldn't try that at home. After the kids were born, I used my maternity underwear as fitted sheets for my king-sized bed.

I grabbed a handful of likely prospects and headed upstairs to a narrow closet with a mirror. The closet was lined with stacks of soft robes in every color. I wanted them all. But I had to be brave, try the bathing suits on. No really, we're talking *piccolissima.* But I found two that had the proper combination of under-wire, figure flattering shape and a small, attached flare gun to direct attention elsewhere. I was all set for the beach, now all I needed was a plastic surgeon, a personal trainer, and a tanning salon.

Then Giovanna showed me the evening wear. She pulled out a long black dress. With beading in all the right places. Spaghetti straps. Okay, it was a gown. A person who stood for three hours every night chopping vegetables did not need a gown, she needed a dependable supply of water, electricity, and a personal chef.

Giovanna beamed. "Try it on!" I did. It was gorgeous. I bought it, to the murmured assent of the lovely Italian ladies in the shop. Women who support the exhilarating purchase of superfluous gowns are an antidote to the horrors of buying a bathing suit. We laughed, we talked about the dress, and they complimented me on my Italian, which was well stocked with effusive superlatives about clothing. When we got home, Giovanna's sister hemmed the dress; it would be ready for our trip to Tenerife.

What a brilliant experience. To find the perfect dress, in 10 minutes, was delightful. To laugh with women in another language was heaven.

Now, all I needed was a yacht with a dance floor, champagne, and tickets to the opera.

Chapter 30
Let's Get This Straight

I continued to foray into the mysteries of ordinary Italian life. How do you get a haircut? One Friday, emboldened by a successful bus ride from Modena's center to the apartment, I decided to give that a whack. My bouffant locks were a mess of Mozartian excess, and I needed to make them small enough to fit on public transportation.

I started with what looked like a relatively non-terrifying salon, and after the hair stylist determined that I knew only enough Italian to ensure that he could attack my hair with impunity, we began. Signore Parrucchiere slashed away at my locks. It was a great cut, and between the shampoo and the brushing, he had transformed what was left of my hair into a mass of healthy curls thick enough to be a pelt. I was impressed, and this spurred him on to greater achievements. As so often happens with people who cut curly hair, Parrucchiere was struck by the realization that what I really wanted was to wear my hair straight. (I don't.) He threw himself into a frenzy of straightening and piling my hair into the shape of a pyramid, so that when he was done, I looked exactly like Christian Siriano, a former *Project Runway* winner. I was FIERCE!!

Grateful for all that had happened up until the Runway 'do, I had planned to tip large and buy products. And then I burrowed into my purse and found just enough money to pay for the cut and a small tip, and since this was in my Debit Debacle phase, I had no access to supplemental plastic. So once again, ONCE AGAIN, a transaction ended in TOTAL EMBARASSMENT. I paid for the cut, but a big tip just wasn't happening, and nevah mind that volumizer, *grazie*.

After the disaster at the first salon, and when I finally had a useable bank card, I found a fabulous hairdresser named Patrizia. She sold me the *only* bottle of shampoo that *ever* made my hair shiny.

Like a bout with airport security[18], I always had to brace myself for a haircut with Patrizia. Stepping into her mango-colored salon, I was enveloped in a creamy mousse of captivating conversation and rich laughter. We laughed about everything women talk about: men, kids, politics, religion. We spoke in rapid Italian, and I was always a few syllables short of full understanding, so with every new topic, my brain veered like an exhilarated kid on *"Mr. Toad's Wild Ride."*

My Italian was coming along nicely. My Italian was perfectly fine. It was when Italians spoke to me that there was a problem. They poured out a million syllables a minute, and I had to sort through the ones I recognized to assemble words. It was a lot like putting together a hand in gin rummy: I put down my three 2s, with a grand and proud flourish, and Patrizia had already gone out with a Ten-Jack-Queen-King-Ace run. And then she dealt another hand... it was exhausting.

But when my appointment was over and I stepped back onto the sidewalk, my heart had been rattled like a maraca, and my crankiness gently fluttered to the pavement, like hair clippings. Patrizia was only hairdresser who ever understood me, and I didn't understand a sizeable chunk of what she was saying.

We were friends, so every time she cut my hair, Patrizia became more invested in passing me off as a real Italian. Although many Italians are born with ebony curls, they do not accept the limitations of nature—they subdue and triumph over it. Italian women defy gravity with fabulous bosoms and stiletto heels; men scoff at summer heat in close-cut wool gabardine suits.

Italians don't covet natural beauty; nature envies the art and allure of Italians.

Italians *manage* their natural resources. They dye their hair in colors on the russet spectrum between copper and Lambrusco. Although Modena had many elderly residents, gray hair was sparse; males and females over 40 tinged their locks to a brickish hue. Younger women opted for a high-gloss pomegranate finish. Their hair sparkled audibly, like wind chimes. But to make it sing, you had to take out the kinks.

Patrizia hoped that I would go burgundy, but her top priority was curl removal. Every visit, as I sank into her swivel chair and faced the mirror, she would plunge her fingers deep into my unruly mop and pull. Then she'd flip

---

18   Tragically, that shampoo was confiscated in an ugly incident involving carry-on luggage and airport security's obsession with essential fluids. I accept the apologies of the flying public, whose safety was secured with 16 ounces of Schwarzkopf's Hair Restorer.

open a pamphlet of hair straightening products. She'd point out their various merits, hoping I'd eventually straighten out.

I demurred but never wavered. Patrizia was so intent on performing a humanitarian service, she wasn't dissuaded. Not until she was sure the pamphlet had convinced me to go straight at my next appointment would she pull out her scissors. She did a wonderful job. When she finished cutting, my hair was wild and tousled, and I looked 20 years younger and impossibly chic. So, I would say, "*Mi piace molto, come questo.*" (I like this a lot, just like this.) But these words merely unleashed a tsunami of wave removal.

In this phase, Patrizia would grab a metal roller brush used to pave highways, trap a ringlet in its bristles, and turn on the blow dryer. The heat was so intense it melted the fillings in my *lower* molars. She dug the bristles into my scalp and pulled so hard my neck would have qualified as Pilates equipment.

When she was done, and all of the waves had been wrenched from my scalp, I didn't look ravishingly Italian, I resembled the Beatles in their "Love Me Do" period. Sometimes I looked like Paul, with impermeable bangs and a mahogany fringe that plummeted to my collar. Carrying a sitar, I would have been mistaken for George. On a stormy day, I approximated Ringo in a wind tunnel.

I am philosophical about my hair because I have often experienced Hairmageddon. In my senior year of high school, I kept my hair short and blew it dry, so for some inexplicable reason, I didn't know that it was curly. I went to a hairdresser in search of a little wave, and was permanently scarred.

That hell beast hairdresser wound my hair into the smallest curling rods, plastered on permanent solution, and left it on my hair for an hour. When she took out the rods, all the fine strands that had formed my bangs broke away, and the remaining frizz seized into a dense mushroom cloud on top of my head. At the time I was short and pudgy, and my physique was arranged in a graduated series of ballish chunks, so with my new 'do, I looked like a snowman attacked by a mushroom cloud. The compassionate souls in my high school called me Poodle, but they were so doubled over with laughter I couldn't make out what else they called me.

This is not the kind of character-building experience that lends itself to greatness, but I certainly kept my perspective on the importance of a Bad Hair Day.

So, when a salon in Boston made me look so much like Hillary Clinton that Bill cheated on me, I responded diplomatically. In Denver, a stylist turned my mop into a helmet; she'd cut my hair into a ball, fluff it into a sphere, and coat it with so much hairspray I'd draw blood breaking through the crust. No worries, it wasn't permanent. And no matter what style I tried, my curls would revert to the same lunatic fringe. After every shampoo, my freak flag flew.

I didn't need a magenta mane to feel Italian all the way to my roots; I love my hair just the way it is. And I loved Patrizia, who made every moment in her chair a dizzying whirl into her world.

She loves you yeah, yeah, yeah...

Chapter 31
Winging It

Bzzzzzz. *"I'm sleeping, and right in the middle of a good dream, when all at once I wake up at something that keeps knocking at my brain…"* Wait. That wasn't knocking, it was the high-pitched whine of another mosquito.

Italian mosquitos are like Italian cars—they're teeny, fast, and loud. But because of their size, getting nailed by *una zanzara* is like getting hit by a Fiat. For all the screeching, there's not much damage. Italian mosquito bites itch for a moment, plump into a welt the size of a pimple, and fade quickly.

Like pamphlets on Italian hair straightening techniques, I had no way to avoid them. Our apartment didn't have window screens, but few buildings did. All those charming photos of Italian streets, with painted shutters flung wide, and geraniums sunning themselves in the windows? No screens. You can't water geraniums if you have to give them a drink through little mesh holes. And you can't drape yourself alluringly onto the sill if you are sealed inside by fine wire mesh.

What if the Capulets had window screens? Romeo would have looked up at Juliet's bedroom and said, "But soft, what light through yonder window breaks? I can hear muttering, but I can't see a thing." Window screens may put more of a damper on young love than the Pope.

Although I searched for Italian screens, I found them only twice. Halfway up the Leaning Tower of Pisa, an opening in a wall was covered with the same thick mesh that surrounded American sun porches of the 1950s. Aha! I'll bet Galileo put that on there. Historians assume that Galileo threw balls from the Tower to test whether objects of different masses fell at different rates. But I think he was trying to kill mosquitos in his courtyard when he discovered it was more efficient to fence them out. This could also explain why Galileo got in trouble with the Catholic Church: along with indulgences, the bishops may have been selling fly swatters, and didn't want the competition.

With Galileo's screen idea squelched, for the next 500 years, the window of opportunity for mosquitos remained wide open, and it still is. While walking through a neighborhood in Parma, I spotted the kind of screens we had in the US. Three identical windows held three American screens—of three different heights. The gap between each screen and window ranged between 6 and 12 inches. Apparently Italian mosquitos aren't good at measuring.

Instead of screens, Italians use retractable slats that slide down over doors and windows. The slats are lowered by a heavy chord. You drop the slat curtain, and then pull up slightly, to expose tiny holes between the strips. The holes are supposed to be too small to let in mosquitos. But they're also too small to let in air molecules. And the slats in our apartment were made of wood, which had warped over time, so the holes were big enough to let in feral badgers.

In desperation, I asked friends what they used for mosquito control. "Try those coils they sell at the supermarket," someone suggested. I remembered those coils from my childhood; they're thick flat punks the color and texture of mustard. You lit the end, then blew it out. Thick, acrid smoke slithered from the smoldering tip, possibly releasing mustard gas. As the room filled with poisonous fog, my kids gagged and disappeared. They didn't make the mosquitos go away, but they worked nicely on children.

Another friend suggested a product sold in the grocery store presciently called Vape, a liquid in a dispenser you plugged into a wall socket; it worked like air freshener, in reverse. Insecticide, warmed in its plastic pot, became airborne, and dropped the teeny varmints in their tracks. But for the Vape to work, we had to seal up the windows and stay out of the house for 12 hours; that made me feel like the mosquitos had won. Besides, I didn't want to live in a No Pest Strip.

With no other workable options, we closed the windows against the winged beasties. With no fresh air, we were trapped in the summer heat with our own fetid funk. Modena's humidity was so thick that water vapor remained aloft and created cumulus clouds around the apartment. Rivers of sweat ran off our faces and stayed airborne at eye level. If someone sneezed, it rained.

I finally asked Melanie, who knows everything, what to do. Her response? Electric fans. Mosquitos are small and can't fly in wind. So we bought fans. I can't tolerate white noise; it masks the soothing gurgle of monsters salivating under my bed. But Annalise's legs were a Braille version of the Gettysburg Address, and when the mosquitos started high-fiving each other when they entered our apartment, it was time to fight back.

So we cranked up the fans. After being pinned to the wall by high winds, I learned it's hard for me to sleep on my side. And like a dog with his tongue hanging out of a moving car, I found I was eating a lot more bugs than usual, but eventually even I became a fan. Or, I could break open a vein and fill the little Vape dispensers with my own blood.

"I'll Meet You Halfway..."

Chapter 32
Bella

When I was too tired of living in Italy without a car, I bought a new bike. Okay, my bike was made just after they laid off the bricklayers at the Colosseum, but it was new for me. She was a beat-up burgundy upright, with a wide seat, a basket in front, and a rack in the back. "Nice rack," said Andy, but I think he was impressed that I could carry groceries. Biking is so good for marriage.

And she had a little bell, so I call her Bella: "Beautiful."

As we rolled along, Bella had something to say about everything we passed. "Someone in the road! DIIING!" "A bit of yellow in that sign! Trrrinnnng!" "Look, flowers!! Brrriiiinngg!"

The incessant chatter distracted me from my biggest priority, staying alive. All the guidebooks say that Modena's city center is closed to auto traffic, but I was dodging bikes, pedestrians, cars, and trucks, and that was just on the sidewalk.

Once we started moving, I learned more about my new friend. Bella had one gear: slow and creaky. At Bella's peak speed, a slug wouldn't break a sweat. But that worked for me. The slower I was going when I was hit by a car, the greater my chances for a full recovery.

Around the time Bella was built, the ancient Romans finished a perfectly straight road, Via Emilia, that stretches 170 miles, from Rimini to Piacenza. Via Emilia was the street Bella learned to ride on, so turning left or right was a modern innovation that didn't interest her. Her brakes worked, but she thought slamming into something was a perfectly reasonable way to stop.

As she hummed along the bike path, Bella chirped to herself, which made everyone look at us. It's hard to look cool on a bike that calls out to everyone in a three-mile radius. "Heeey—nice shoes there." "Is that a new perfume?" "Where'd you get that scar?" People were getting annoyed. To keep from getting clubbed like a baby seal, I muffled the bell with my hand. That made it harder to work the handbrake, but there was plenty to hit in Italy; I'd stop.

Modena's bike paths run beside the vehicular madness known as Italian roads. To keep cars off the bike paths, the city installed squat concrete posts. The posts are too close together to let cars through, but they're so close they barely let bicycles through either, and they're everywhere. By the time I registered that a concrete barrier was approaching, I was about to hit it straight on, which would have been fine except for Bella's turning and brake issues. We had some things to work out.

But we took a glorious ride to the supermarket, and I was able to carry home groceries a lot faster than if I were walking. On the way home, Bella got quiet. Her rack and her basket were full, and we were outside of the city center where a pedestrian was hit by a car just days before. There was no bike path on that risky road, and it was a tense ride.

As I pulled into traffic, a tough biker chick—a *nonna* with at least 70 years under her billowing widow's weeds—pulled up behind me. She wanted to pass, but the only available space was occupied by a homicidal Fiat on my left, and a pedestrian on my right. She was gaining and I had no good options: I had to choose between taking the high road or becoming the low road. She inched closer, but I held my ground. She downshifted and hit her bell, hard: "DIIIINNNG!" In Italy, a bike bell and the opening bell at a boxing match serve the same purpose: "Gloves Up!!"

I tried to remain cool; this woman was at least 75, and if she got me in a headlock, I'd be toast. I needed to fend her off from behind while facing all of the hazards of Modena traffic: perilous potholes, manic motorcycles, pugilistic pigeons. It was Mad Maxx Geriatric Edition, but one of us had an unfair muscular advantage: she was wearing support hose. She was creeping so close I could feel the steam rising off her unnaturally auburn scalp, and here it came again:

"DDDDIIIINNNNNG!!"

Bella, who was so quiet she was a dead ringer for a dead ringer, sprang to my defense. She spit right back. "DIIIIIINNNNNNG!!!! Back off or eat pavement, Babe!!" I cringed, expecting a volley of expletives, but Signora Nemesis dropped away. Now there was only the wind at my back and Bella trilling softly: We won.

Good friends know when to let it ride and when to take your side. I had the most beautiful friend in the world: *Grazie mille*, Bellissima.

Chapter 33
It Happens

It does happen. For all the joking about lunatic Italian drivers, they seemed to be making some inroads on the pedestrian population. We lived above a traffic circle, and the street usually whirred with Fiats and Smart Cars and bicyclists and trucks. Sometimes the trucks were comically small, with a single wheel in the front, two in the back; they looked like cars from Richard Scarry's animal towns. Sirens shrieked hysterically as they responded to the latest crisis. And I always wondered, as I entered the crosswalk, whether I'd make it to the other side without being snuffed into the pavement like a cigarette.

One day, after more than the usual noise from the traffic circle, I saw a car accident in the final, bureaucratic stages of cleanup. There were a few police vehicles blocking off the area, and a lone car with an ominous hood concavity. Because only one car was surrounded by police tape, I assumed that the car had hit a pedestrian. When the police were through, two marks indicated the position of the car's wheels, and a circle on the concrete pinpointed the impact zone.

It happened.

As I waited beside the crosswalk for traffic to clear, honking drivers careened around the accident scene, hurtling toward me. Why slow down just because someone may have died?

One morning only days later I was brushing my teeth with the window open. There was a surge of sound, I felt desperate wheels straining to spread rubber over the road, and a dull thud. Three beats of silence, and then a scream. *Oh, no, someone's been hit by a car.*

There was deep moaning, and a woman yelled, "BAMBIIIINNNAAAA!"

I climbed to the roof. A dessicated blonde, doughish in drapey blue-gray polyester, stood in front of a little green car whose dull paint was faded to a sickly shade of pea. Behind the car, tucked against the curb, was a rectangular yellow bus, neatly compact like the mauve one my kids rode to school. The bus driver wore a crisp blue uniform; fortunately, his bus was empty. Out of the little car tumbled a bloated woman with burgundy hair; she was probably the driver's sister.

In front of the car, screened from my view by a tree, was the pedestrian, who was still lying in the road. I hoped it wasn't a child.

I was amazed by two things: how long it took the driver to light her first cigarette, and how long it took the police to send a single squad car.

In the US, an injured pedestrian would have required the assistance of at least one fire truck, a rescue vehicle, an ambulance or three, and five police cars. For accidents, we "cop up." Here, a rescue vehicle discreetly pulled off to the side, rescue workers hunched over the victim, and the ambulance arrived and silently parked behind them. There was a lot of discussion about the best way to lift the patient. Finally, a backboard was placed on top of the gurney, and the poor woman, her neck secured by a brace, was lifted into the ambulance.

The ambulance left without using the siren, which made me wonder what all the other rescue vehicles were screeching about. The victim was taken to a hospital, where her treatment was funded by tax dollars. At home, if the pedestrian were uninsured, the hospital would lose a fortune treating her. If she were insured, she'd lose months, and maybe her house, fighting about what treatment she deserved. Also, responding to accidents costs Modena a lot less than at home. Why all the fuss about socialized medicine? It cuts way down on emergency vehicle traffic.

The victim was taken away, and still the police hadn't arrived. Finally, a single car labeled *Polizia Municipale* pulled up and discharged three thin cops. In the States, the officers would be steroidally beefy and swaggering with testosterone; they'd have their whirling lights flashing, and the radio would be blaring with calls for backup. But the Modena officers were no more imposing than the bus driver. They listened to the bus driver and the woman who hit the pedestrian.

There was a lot of arm waving from the participants, but there was no real disagreement over what happened; the car driver was trying to pass the bus on the left when she struck a woman crossing the street. This wouldn't end well for the drivers. The cops conferred at the back of their police car, a streamlined hatchback. It was hot standing in the street, so the two women sat on the curb, and the blonde curled into herself and cried. The other woman sat silently and didn't raise a hand in comfort.

The cops measured and discussed and drew marks on the road, and the women waited. The bus driver was issued a citation, and as he walked past, he leaned down to give each woman a gentle clutch. Finally, the cops finished the paperwork, and the women got back in their car. As the driver's sister slowly edged back into traffic, other vehicles scuffed the chalk marks from the accident not yet over, and horns protested her unexpected hesitancy.

It happens. Maybe Italians wonder about why it happens in Italy so often, and Americans wonder why it ends in America so badly.

Chapter 34
Foreigner

Just when I was adjusting to being unsettled, Andy left for five days to give a presentation in the United States, and I was alone in Modena with the kids. To be a single parent of my children for more than an hour was unnerving. To do it in a foreign country, with no car, no real grasp of what was covered under our health insurance, and a huge fear that I would have to find out, was even scarier than buying pants.

People scoff at "it takes a village," but when you are *una straniera*, "a foreigner," having a social network is a matter of survival. In the US we had excellent insurance, specialists, and pediatricians down the street, but in Italy, we had cellphones that sometimes worked[19] and an American doctor who lived in Bologna. I could call him in a medical emergency, but we may have had different definitions of what that meant. "Dr. Williams? We have no milk for tea, and no drinking water, and I can't carry milk and six liters of water at the same time. Obviously, I can't live without caffeine. How soon can you be here??"

I had a list of emergency numbers on the fridge, including the phone numbers for our friends who lived nearby, Elena and Edward. And Melanie, who lived 100 miles away but could magically produce an ATM card from Milan, was critical to our survival. Although Melanie said we could dial #118 to summon an ambulance, Italian ambulances prowled the public squares trolling for patients. I didn't know whether to be comforted that EMTs were so eager to serve, or freaked that they knew something I didn't. Either way, I wasn't sure what happened after you dialed #118, so I tried to avoid allowing the children to spurt blood or break bones.

I'm an attorney, and lawyers analyze every situation to determine All of the Things That Can Go Wrong. For example, when I said, "Don't climb on that wall," and my seven-year-old asked, "Why not?" I gave an excruciatingly detailed

---

19   I thought they were called "cell phones" because I usually ended up talking to myself.

explanation of the potential consequences for every misstep. "If you climb on that wall while your brother is standing next to you on his bike, he's going to bump into you and you're going to pitch forward and split your head open on the dirty concrete, which will result in a concussion, stitches, and quite possibly a dangerous infection. In the alternative, you're going to reel backward, fall into that rose bush, and we'll be picking thorns out of your ribs for the next three weeks. If the medical care is negligent, you'll spend years in depositions, may have to testify against the doctor, and for all your trouble, you probably won't see a dime."

The threat of depositions always stopped her cold. It's good to have a variety of parenting tools at the ready; how do doctors keep *their* kids off walls?

I wouldn't have been so nervous about blood loss if we weren't still in health care limbo. After the horrific visit to the Questura, we were still waiting for our appointment to finalize our Permesso Di Soggiorno. The Permesso may have entitled us to Italian health insurance cards, which for me would have included a ghastly ID photo that would have ensured me immediate access to emergency care.

Delays in receiving a Permesso were common. Some students from Andy's university spent their whole junior year in Bologna. Within days of their arrival, the American students reported to the Questura to apply for their residency permits, but often the Permesso wasn't granted for many months, sometimes not until after the students left. And then a new batch of students was dispatched to the Questura.[20]

The futility of processing documents for the Italian government must take its toll. Maybe that's where mimes come from. But to wait for a document until you no longer need it is as Italian as the creamy swirl of gelato. Yet for every bureaucratic inconvenience, there was delicious compensation.

For example, while waiting patiently for the Permesso in Modena's square, I enjoyed a spectacular buffet lunch with Elena. The restaurant was beside a bell tower that tilts slightly away from an ancient church, which also leans, but in the other direction. The bell tower, Ghirlandina, was new, only 700 years old. For 700 years, those bells have warned Modenese of fires, approaching invaders, and passing hours. I was once inside the tower when the bells went off: deep sonorous notes reverberated against the sun and sky. Take your time, Questura. I could wait.

---

20   We never received our Permesso. Was there a malfunction in the filing system at Sportello Number Four?

The tower looms beside Modena's Duomo, an 800-year-old cathedral. We were once in the Duomo at the beginning of 10 o'clock Mass. The priest sang the Mass in Italian accompanied by a choir of angels; the notes of the organ soared against the ancient stone. I fiercely wanted to hear the Christmas service in a church that had celebrated not only Pavarotti's life, but the birth of Jesus—804 times. Our artist friend Piero's paintings of the Duomo capture every flicker of light, every shadow, every shade, of that infinitely beautiful stone. And, during a tour of the interior, he showed me a hinged wooden shelf that folded out to face the congregation: the executioner's seat. That kept the parishioners focused on the sermon.

In the piazza near the Duomo lies a slab of granite, larger than a tomb. Now it holds students cradling laptops, but for 900 years, this stone held public speakers and public executions.

Italian efficiency is a marvelous thing.

My two-hour lunch with Elena ended blissfully, with a cappuccino. Drinking milk with coffee after 10:30 is heresy for Italians, so to have an afternoon cappuccino marks you as *una straniera*. But the hourglass was running down, Toto, and Auntie Em makes awful coffee.

Let's have one for the road.

On my way home from lunch, I stopped at an optician's office to get some saline. It was closed. Chiuso. I pulled and pushed the door. *Niente.* I stepped back to read the dizzying array of small clocks designating the store's hours. Open at 9, closed at 1, open at 3:30, closed at 6. There were still a lot of clocks left to read, so that was only Monday's schedule. While I was still deciphering the little hands, a man opened the door from the inside.

He was tall, with a rag wrapped around his splayed gray hair. He wore a bulging black t-shirt with faded silver lettering that staggered across the globe of his stomach. He looked more like a pirate than an optician, and he spoke in rapid Italian. I was a few *arrghhs* behind, so I didn't understand what he said, but since he held the door open, I asked if I could buy some saline.

"E' giovedì pomeriggio," he explained, with the mournful tones of an official announcement of the death of a head of state. *"E' giovedì pomeriggio."* We shook our heads in unison: It is Thursday afternoon, when most of Modena is closed. The fact that it was also closed Monday morning, all day Sunday, and a million national holidays does not seem to diminish the need to close on Thursday afternoon. He asked if I were from Modena, implying that only una straniera would approach a Modena shop door on Thursday afternoon. He could probably smell the cappuccino on my breath, another sign of stranierosity.

"Sono Americana," I responded, and we had reached complete understanding: Americans did not know about Thursday afternoon.

In Colorado, I can buy saline at Costco, enough to create a saltwater aquarium, on Thursday afternoon. I can try on clothes. I wait hours, not months or years, for government documents. But I cannot drink cappuccino beside an 800-year-old church with assigned seating for an executioner, and I cannot speak to a pirate in Italian. *Arrrrrgh.*

Chapter 35
Game On

In Italy we didn't have a television, but we knew when the local soccer teams were playing because we could hear cheers and expletives from every window. Andy couldn't pass up a chance to see a game in person, so we bought tickets for a match between Bologna and Genoa.

Even outside the arena, the Italian obsession with security made me a little insecure. Walking to the stadium entrance, we passed a van full of *Carabinieri,* (Italian military police) who looked ready for a medium-sized war. Unlike the relatively peaceful *Polizia Municipale*, (city cops) who look and dress like bus drivers, Carabinieri are heavily armed. The jauntiness of their berets was off-set by the lethality of their weapons—machine guns and military pistols. And their rigid faces conveyed the reassuring warmth of a freshly launched ballistic missile.

But the van guards were just the vanguard. Most of the parking spots on the street next to the stadium were taken by the vehicles of Polizie and Carabinieri. It felt like we had tickets to a civil war.

At the Bologna stadium, fans were allowed to enter only through the door closest to our seats. We handed our tickets and passports to a smiling matron in a bullet-proof booth, who slid the bar codes over a super-cool *007-esque* glass panel. That released a high-tech yet medieval revolving door: an iron pole studded with steel spikes. When the spikes swung shut, we were sealed inside the stadium with the soccer fans, and the military and municipal police who were determined to stop the fans from doing whatever the authorities expected them to do.

What fun?

The stadium held 39,000 people. The seating arrangements were slightly more modern than the Roman Coliseum: the chairs were molded plastic fanny-rests glued onto gray concrete.

In addition to soccer, the stadium hosted track and field events, so the soccer field sat inside a ring of running track. Positioned all along the track were security guys who wore bright yellow vests and construction hats and sat on buckets to watch the crowd for signs of trouble. Security guys were also posted all the way up the steps in all four quadrants of the stadium. Under the vests, they wore street clothes; next week, those same guys would be looking for a fight, but from slightly more comfortable seats.

The game had already started, and because soccer is played in two 45-minute halves with no chance to stop the clock, unlike American sporting events, this game would end on time. Limiting the games to 90 minutes must save the Italians a fortune on overtime expenses for all those cops. Italians use the extra money to fund socialized medicine, so they can provide free medical care to guys who get hurt in fights that break out as soon as the police leave. Italian soccer is very efficient.

Italian soccer is leagues apart from American baseball. The most startling difference was the relative silence. American sports fans are bombarded by a constant wall of sound. There's a booming announcer, a leering organ, pulses of music, calls to "*MMMAAAAKKKKKE SSOOOOOOOOMMMMME NNNOOOOOOIIIIIISSSSSE!!!!*" Every time a baseball player passes gas, the Jumbotron blares with his lifetime stats and maudlin backstory. Vendors constantly cajole the crowd to buy food and drinks. American baseball fans are never left alone long enough to realize that they spend six hours and $130 to watch men mostly stand around and scratch their man parts. Don't we get enough of that at home?

This game was eerily quiet. In the soccer stadium, the only time the announcer spoke was when he announced a score or a penalty. Occasionally the score board chimed gently to announce a score from another game. But otherwise, the fans were left to their own devices.

With no sports-o-tainment, Bologna fans just watched the game. There were no mindless color-coded races of a sponsor's product. "*Which coooooolor Haaaaaarley will wiiiinnnn????*" There were no roving cameras to catch fans watching themselves on the Jumbotron. There were no mascots, no naked beer-barrel guys, no huge foam fingers waving maniacally. No *waaaaves*. Or announcer-led song fests, or even half-time shows. Weirdly, Italians go to a soccer match to be entertained by… soccer.

And these fans didn't eat themselves into a stupor. We arrived 20 minutes into the first half, and when we sat down, I didn't see anyone near us eating or drinking. Anything. In an American stadium, at any point in a game, about a third of the fans are walking to and from their seats, on a quest to consume or de-consume vats of food and drink. But in the Bologna soccer stadium, the whole time the players were on the field, fans remained seated. At half-time, about 40 percent of the fans got up, to avoid a cop, or to visit the snack bar. But Italians were in search of just a snack: three ounces of food or drink. Or less.

US stadiums are ringed with restaurants that serve heart-stopping fast food of every description, but not Bologna's. One vendor that served only Coke in small paper cups had one of those clump o' customers that make Americans wonder why Italians can't form lines like regular people. Andy and the kids found another stand, with a real line, that sold Coke and a snack product called Stella Chips. Stella Chips were made from fried potatoes molded into a ruffled disc the size and shape of a crenellated Catholic Host. And that's how they tasted, but maybe those were the ones they sold on Sunday.

There was a family seated in front of me. At halftime, the dad braved the snack bar. He brought back food for himself, his wife, his parents, and his eight-year-old son.

Five people shared:

Two sodas,

a box of fried Host, and

a small bag of pistachios.

They finished the chips, ate half the pistachios, and re-sealed the bag.

On my left, two burly guys plowed through:

A drink each,

a single box of fried Hosts, and

a small ice cream cone.

Americans would starve at a Bologna soccer match.

The Italian fans didn't watch themselves kiss or wave, or eat, they watched the game, and at least half of them got mad. The Bologna fans were infuriated because they were losing; clearly that was an affront to both their civic pride and their manhood. In response, the Genovese waved their manhoods at the Bolognese, clearly a dick move. I don't think the Bologna fans appreciated that.

Seated next to us was a squat man whose face and scalp were a single roiling scab of boiled skin that unhinged at the jaw to let him scream. Sitting silently beside Signore *Bollente*, (Boiling) was his teenaged son, a studious-looking boy who wrapped his scarf around his face to protect himself from streams of cigarette smoke, or maybe flying spittle, from his crazed father.

Signor Bollente followed every moment of the game and was enraged by most of it. He yelled at the refs, the players, and the Genovese. At one point, he fell two rows into the seats below us, but he got right back up and started shouting again. He used all the swear words I had learned from my dad as a toddler. In a moment of unexpected sweetness, a Bolognese fan in his twenties turned to shake his head at the crazy man. We exchanged looks and started laughing. "*What's up with that guy?*"

Italian soccer fans didn't boo to express anger, they whistled like a million deranged teakettles. But to me, their anger sounded like cheering. I *so* don't understand sports.

Instead of foam fingers, the Italians waved flags. Huge, majestic ones, red and blue for the Bolognese, a yellow shield on a blue background for the Genovese. The banners rippled gracefully across the stands. Beneath the fluttering flags, there was singing. These songs were mournfully lyrical, songs about home. The teams for both fans sounded like soldiers on their way to war. Deep voices joined and ready for battle seemed a tad more dignified than the Denver Bronco's naked barrel guy belting out, "*Hey, Baby… I wanna knoooow, will you be my girl…*"

Bologna was losing, Genoa was gloating, and as the game came to a close, I wondered about all those cops. Was all that force necessary? Then I saw that the Genoa fans were held inside what could only be described as a cage. The visitors' section was fenced in by iron mesh walls 20 feet high, a shoulder-high barrier was topped by steel spikes, and an unbroken line of security guys blocked access to the entrance.

And then I understood that all the precautions were meant for the moment when somebody loses and somebody wins, when the fans meet outside, and those mournful city songs are still ringing in everyone's ears. Unlike American sports fans, Italian soccer fans have met not just on the field of dreams, but on the field of battle. Italy has been unified only since 1861. For hundreds of years, Italian city-states were at war; for centuries, men from these same towns raped and pillaged and fought to the death. That's why my name and passport number were printed on my ticket, that's why the visiting team was caged, and that's why the Carabinieri were prepared for combat: they were ready for fans who forgot it was just a game.

As Signor Bollente and his son walked past the jeering Genovese, the teen-ager hurled his paper cup at the steel mesh wall. For his sake, I was glad that the Carabinieri were waiting outside.

Chapter 36
Race for the Cure

The Race for the Cure raises breast cancer awareness and money for research, all over the world. In 2009 Italy held one in nearby Bologna. If any country has an interest in maintaining the health of breasts, it's Italy. Mother Nature would be proud that Italy is out front in protecting such an impressive natural resource.

Bologna was only 30 minutes from Modena by train, but to get there required a 90-minute transport trifecta of private enterprise, public transit, and brute force. Modena's buses don't run early on Sunday morning, so we took a cab to the train station, and then a train to Bologna. In front of the train station, the bus stops were meticulously labeled for each of the routes. We confidently waited at the designated stop for our bus, Number 33. Of course, that bus pulled up on the opposite side of the square, and we had to run like lunatics to catch it. How Italians maintain their cool in the face of incessant institutional anarchy escapes me.

In Bologna, a bus ride cost one euro. Bus company employees boarded the busses, checking for tickets. Failure to show a ticket could result in a 30-euro fine. Children rode free, but the definition of "child" seemed to vary, from 10 to 13 years old. Alex was 13, but his height and feral red mop pushed him well past the child fare mark. With only two euro coins between us, Andy and I prepared to agree with the authorities that Alex really needed a ticket *and* a haircut.

Andy already had his race t-shirt and runner number. But we needed to get the rest of us in gear. Within minutes, we each had our shirts, racing numbers, and heavy burlap gift bags stuffed with free samples. Alex's and mine were loaded with mouthwash and sunscreen; Annalise's had fun kid stuff and black licorice that tasted so much like tar I actually wanted to use the Listerine.

Andy had signed us up for the noncompetitive race because competition brings out the best in Italians, and who wanted to deal with that? Competing with a spandex-clad Italian engaged in any sport is like lining up against a Ferrari in a Formula 1 car race. We heard that the Italian leader of a Formula 1 race team had recently ordered a driver to crash his car so another driver on the same team could win. You certainly wouldn't want *that* kind of thing in a mini marathon.

Around 10-ish, the noncompetitive racers ambled over to the starting line. A gun was fired, and several minutes later, we shuffled forward. Apparently, we all were competing to be the last to start the race.

Eventually Andy and the kids bolted for the finish line, leaving me to hold their swag. I used to run seven to ten miles a day, for no apparent reason. But before Alex was born, I snapped my calf muscle during the Boulder Bolder 10K, and whenever I run, it threatens to tear again. So I was happy to walk the course.

And oh, what a course. The race started in the Giardini Margherita, a park that looked like the parks at home, except it was full of gorgeous people speaking Italian and wearing amazing shoes. The walkers sashayed out of the park and strolled along streets lined with portici, some of them covered in frescoes from the Middle Ages. Above the portici were arched and shuttered windows framed by finely etched columns right out of the balcony scene in *Romeo and Juliet*. The sidewalks beneath the portici were softly colored and polished marble, but at eye level the walls blared with graffiti. I hardly noticed; I spent most of my walk time swiveling between the frescoes and the fabulous shoes.

We made our way along Via Santo Stefano. The street meandered sinuously, and the buildings leaned companionably together, so even a mini marathon was a dreamy reverie.

We passed familiar Bologna landmarks like the Neptune Fountain, where the gloriously muscled God of the Sea holds his trident high above his surging torso, bulging thighs, and manly buttocks. Below him, at the base of the fountain, luscious mermaids flaunted their breasts, and their cups literally over-flowed. These ladies raise breast awareness every single day.

After Neptune we ambled past Bologna's Wall of the Partigiani, a display of 2,000 photos of men and women who gave their lives defending Bologna from Nazis and Fascists in World War II. These photographs, with the heroes' eyes blazing with the passion of their sacrifice, light up public squares all over Italy.

Minutes later, we reached Santo Stefano, a cluster of ancient churches, the oldest built in 460 A.D. One of the churches has a dome that's not covered with paint or plaster, so you could see how a pile of rectangular bricks becomes a smoothly curved hemisphere.

Between the churches was a roughly cobbled courtyard. In the spring, graduating students gather here to celebrate with friends and family. Graduates wear wreaths of laurel leaves that flutter with ribbons, placards that announce their degree, and silly and risqué costumes. They pop champagne corks while their beaming parents look on. One afternoon we watched a group of friends hold a jousting match with cardboard horses, swords, and a giggling maiden who dramatically dipped her scarf to begin the contest. I think she won.

We passed the tombs of four professors who taught law in Bologna in the 13th century. The tombs are marble sarcophagi, set on high thin pillars, and carved with scenes of university life from 800 years ago. Italian law students told me it takes an eternity to get an Italian law degree; some of the original scholars may still be working on it.

Parked at an angle, a row of sleek motorcycles awaited their next adventure. On the cobblestones a silver Ferrari napped in the sun, throwing off daggers of sunlight from paint so rich the finish simmered.

We passed the Torre degli Asinelli, one of 100 defensive brick towers that warring Italian families built in the Middle Ages to protect themselves from other warring Italian families. The Assinelli tower has more than 500 rickety wooden steps that are best climbed in the swelter of August with two kids who think that plummeting 300 feet to their deaths, or making their mother think she will, is a good way to pass an afternoon. Next to the Asinelli is the Torre Garisenda, a leaning tower that Dante mentioned in the *Divine Comedy*.

As I walked, I thought about a question casually asked by a young friend: was I walking in anyone's name? That's a painful question, because cancer not only runs in my family; it hunts down and kills my relatives relatively quickly. My grandmother survived two years. Before she died, she endured surgery, chemo, a colostomy, and radiation, her thin skin cold against the icy metal of the radiation table. My mother was diagnosed with arthritis in her hip, but afraid of a death like her mother's, she ignored her steadily worsening pain. When she finally agreed to exploratory surgery, her hip had already rotted away from cancer. Ten weeks after my mother's diagnosis, we held her funeral; I was nine months pregnant, and two weeks later, I held my son. My cousin Cornelia had a normal OB/GYN exam in March, was diagnosed with ovarian cancer in April, and in May, she was gone. My grandmother lived to be 80, my mom died at 64, and my cousin at 40. And yet I have friends who have fought breast cancer and won.

I walked in everyone's name; I walk because I can.

I walked through paradise. We looped past San Petronio on the Piazza Maggiore, a hulking beast of a cathedral whose grandeur was designed to rival St. Peter's in Rome, but before construction was completed the Pope cut off funding (some scholars say he was offended by the Neptune fountain), leaving its striped pink and white marble facade unfinished. The exposed red brick of its upper half looks rough and lumpish, like a coarsely knit sweater.

We doubled back past the Via dell'Archiginnasio. Tucked into two streets here are a fish market where the fish glimmer like Ferraris, and vegetable and fruit stands where the produce glitters in crystal shades of amethyst, magenta, vermillion, and sunlit lime.

There were no water stations on the course but in the last stretch, a runner, sleek and cool in a slim-fitting white tracksuit, stopped at the edge of the street. With his back to the crowd he stretched out his arm, looked behind him, and offered a drink and a smile to his identically dressed wife. She threw back her head and laughed as she passed and grabbed from his fingers the tiny porcelain cup: he held out a drink of espresso.

At the end of the course, I found my family. We stood with hundreds of other racers to celebrate. The loudspeakers played Melissa Etheridge's Race song, "I Run for Life." Above the crowd, pink and white balloons bobbed and swayed against the clear sky. We all cheered for the race winners, whippets in their 20s who would no doubt bounce off the stage and light cigarettes. The announcer asked everyone holding balloons to release them at the same time. Fumbling for my camera, I missed the moment. But I won't forget a step of that lovely walk, on behalf of the family I lost, for my friends who won, and for the women who today and tomorrow will benefit from breast cancer research.

We all win, not because we walk, or run, but just because we live. Congratulations to you, too.

Part II
Travel Stories

Although every day in Modena was an adventure, in that year we traveled to dozens of 50 European cities, by either train or low-cost airlines, which left me confused in several languages. For example, when we were in Brussels, while Andy was at a conference, I took the kids on the train to Mini-Europe, a theme park based on small-scale reproductions of European landmarks like Estonia's ancient city center, and a five-foot-high Eiffel Tower.

The signs in the Belgian train station were in French and Flemish, not my best languages. Worse, when we stopped for lunch, the theme park's restaurant looked exactly like a Mexican restaurant in Colorado, with carved benches and tables, and faux-Mexican décor.

I felt eerily like I was back in the suburbs of Lakewood. While I had literally come a long way from the days when I was afraid to leave the apartment, I was so worried I'd get us lost on the return trip to Brussels, I wanted to stay in that restaurant forever, eating enchiladas that tasted just like home but were mysteriously topped with mayonnaise.

Travel for me involves equal parts laughter, fear, and exhilaration. Here are some of my favorite travel memories—of Cinque Terre, Venice, Wales, Paris, and a hilariously heinous London hotel.

Chapter 37
Cover Me

Seven months into our Italian Adventure, we'd taken some casualties. In Cinque Terre, a set of gorgeous villages strung along the Ligurian coast, Alex sliced his foot. His cuts plumped up and oozed like a fetid frank, and to a vegetarian, that was the wurst.

Now that he was 13 and his foot was no longer under warranty, we considered amputation. But we had just bought him a new package of socks and wanted to make good on our investment, so we made him soak it and apply antibacterial spray.

Doused in antiseptic, the bacteria hissed and melted away like the Wicked Witch after a sponge bath. Phew.

Why didn't we take him to the doctor? In case of an emergency, we could call Dr. Williams, an American doctor who lived in Bologna, a half-hour train ride away. The kids had a wonderful pediatrician, but to reach her would require 30 minutes on the train and another 20 minutes on the bus. By the time we got him there, he'd either grow a foot, or lose one.

We were in a weird insurance limbo, so we paid for doctor visits in cash. There were local clinics and ERs, but who knew what that would cost? Without a *Permesso,* we couldn't access free medical care.[21] We had private insurance that covered us internationally, but what it covered us *for* was a mystery.

So, we handled injuries with an arsenal of Tylenol, a small bottle of anti-bacterial spray, and several verses of *"Que Sera, Sera."*

The day Alex hurt his foot, I blew out something in my left leg. My thigh swelled, and it hurt mightily. But we were in Cinque Terre, where architecture, nature and scrumptious seafood compete to make you cry. There are houses stacked on houses, in gelato colors, reached by tiny winding steps of stone. The

---

21   Maybe we never received our Permesso because the Italian government was holding a grudge about the cost of the firefighters and bucket truck.

water is aquamarine glass, clear and deep. I had no time for agony. There were stairs to climb, and long walks on cliffs bordering the Ligurian Sea.[22]

Liguuuuurian. Seeeeeea.

I wanted to wrap it around me like a crystal cloak, and I did: I floated in emerald laced with silver, and the fish frolicking just beyond my toes spoke Italian. Swelling, schmelling.

For the rest of the day my leg pain was outvoted by the rest of my senses, which were trying to decide which to swoon over, the stunning views, or the spinach ravioli in a creamy tomato sauce flakey with smoked salmon. With a rabid shark affixed to my thigh bone, I would have continued to smile.

Later that evening, we took several trains home, which involved dragging my aching muscle and my overloaded suitcase up and down several million stairs. The next day, when we finally stopped moving, my leg was on fire.

Fortunately, I had access to the best medical care our international insurance could buy: I looked up leg injuries on the Internet. I researched various leg parts, and what happens when you harm them, and concluded I had blown a muscle in my thigh. Ignoring the injury caused everything else to, in medical terms, go kablooie.

In keeping with the treatment information available to me, most of which was delivered by my friends over Facebook, I kept my leg elevated, iced it, and watched to see whether it would get better or fall off.

---

22   When we asked our Italian artist friend Piero for travel recommendations, he said: "Cinque Terre." I Americaned: "Great. Where else?" He Italianed: "Cinque Terre." I replied, "And after that?" "Cinque Terre." Piero was right, all three times.

My treatment plan was flawless, except for the icing and staying off it parts. Helloooo, Italians don't *do* ice. In the blaze of summer, Italians are relentlessly cool in sweater sets and impeccably pressed wool suits. They are too *cool* for ice. They don't sell it in stores, they don't make it at home, and people with dubious insurance needed to get over that.

I had ice cube trays I bought at the open-air market, but they produced single-cell ice chips. In the undulating heat waves of our apartment, the chips melted as I lurched from the refrigerator to the couch. I had an entire leg to freeze, and sandwich bags that left pools of water in my wake. Not cool. Fortunately, a Facebook friend suggested I try a bag of frozen peas.

We had two whole bags, but when you have no car, a teenaged boy, and a constant need to buy groceries, the decision to sacrifice a food item was harder to make than a pot of risotto. I had to make a choice: Give peas a chance, or crawl north until I found an ice floe. I seized a bag of peas and applied it to my leg. Who needs an orthopedist?

I had ice, but the second part of my treatment plan, resting, was problematic. Only Andy, Alex, and I could carry groceries the quarter-mile home from the grocery store; the three of us eyed with suspicion anyone who claimed to be unfit for a walk to the market. When one of us was wounded, life in the apartment took on all the *bonhomie* of the Donner Party. I had to get back in the traces or I'd have been issued a one-way invitation to dinner. Hoping to avoid a fatal test of family loyalty, I settled the peas on my leg and listened for signs of trouble, like the opening of a bottle of steak sauce.

The peas cooled my leg, and then warmed into a comforting bag of pea soup. When the smell became offensive, I boldly claimed the second bag. With that, the pain receded, and the vultures at the foot of the couch shuffled back a few paces. The kids, who had been asking probing questions about the contents of my life insurance policy, grew resigned to their two-parent status.

A few days later, I could walk without screaming, at least when the kids weren't blaring *Guitar Hero*. (I was developing an allergic reaction to Ozzie Osbourne, but that was a separate issue.) We were back to a three-mule family.

And then Andy attacked an innocent suitcase in a train station. One minute he was reading the Departures board, and the next his toenail was ripped like a cheap piece of Formica. Blood was involved, and fainting, but the fainting part was just me.

Although my grandmother and aunt were both RNs, I do not have the Nursing Gene. I once got woozy when my sister Paula described how her Saint Bernard, 150 pounds of determined stupidity, wrapped her metal chain around Paula's fingers, and bolted. Paula described blood blisters and popping fingernails, and then the room started to go gray.

Worse, in a traumatic vacuum cleaner injury, I once rolled an upright over my toe. That actually did suck, and led to the surgical removal of my toenail. When my podiatrist had completed the nail extraction, he recommended that I check out his fancy footwork. I demurred, explaining that if I looked at my toe, I'd either faint or blow chunks.

Podiatrists are *not* good listeners.

"You really need to see it," he insisted.

To his disgust I *didn't* faint; toed him so.

So taking a hard look at Andy's foot wasn't going to happen. But I asked, every four seconds, whether it was bleeding, or if the toe had developed pus, or gangrene, or scurvy. I like to think these requests for updates were a comfort to my spouse. Message: I cared.

As a vegetarian, I posed no danger to my sweetie in his weakened condition. I love him, and I also had an intense interest in his return to health. Wounded, he couldn't carry groceries, or the huge bottles of water we relied on for drinking, or go pick up the pizza on Fridays from *Pizza Ragno* around the corner. Our odds of survival plummeting, I looked for signs of recovery without actually looking. And he... heeled.

But then I woke up with a new leg thing: my upper thigh sprouted a small angry blister, surrounded by a huge red circle. The whole area was raised, hot and painful. Of course, I sought medical assistance on the Internet.

Half the web sites suggested that it was no big deal, as if discovering a crop circle on my leg visible from space wasn't a cause for alarm. More pessimistic sites predicted I would die within minutes, in which case there wasn't much point in trying to see Dr. Williams in Bologna or going to an ER I couldn't afford.

Further research revealed that I had either a harmless spider bite, a poisonous spider bite, or a serial-killeresque bacteria that would devour my flesh with audible chomping. Two out of three of those options were fatal.

To determine my fate, I needed to scroll through spider bite web sites and play "Match That Wound." I faint at the mere description of afflictions, and the arachnid injury web sites displayed 3D gore. Even worse, photos of gelatinous flesh studded with glistening maggots reminded me of office potluck desserts.

I refused to die with *that* image in my head, so I turned off the computer and hoped there was time for one last cup of gelato.

Que Sera, Sera...

Chapter 38
Venice

We went to Venice for a long weekend. Venice is insanely expensive, so we stayed in a nearby town, just to save a few hundred thousand euros. When we got to the hotel, we were asked for our passports. Italian law required every hotel to register every guest with the local police. Technically, even friends who stayed for more than three days in a private house were required to register. If illustrators had taken this approach, we would never have lost track of Waldo. But for everyone else, it seemed like overkill.

Every time we checked into an Italian hotel, a clerk had to fill out a form with our names and passport numbers. Often the hotel held on to the passports, so the clerk could fill out the paperwork at night, when he wasn't so busy, or when that guy who buys stolen passports stopped by.

The little forms were supposed to deter terrorism, or maybe tourism. *Every* guest, every friend, every stay, every time? How often did police officials read those forms? Wouldn't they read the form only *after* someone had…? Nevah mind.

When asked for our passports, Andy and I were embarrassed; we had forgotten them. Because we weren't crossing borders or meeting with foreign operatives, we were staying for two nights in a cheap hotel outside of Venice. Europeans have identification cards and are accustomed to showing them for every transaction. Americans, who are paranoid that our passports will be stolen and we'll be locked in a Turkish prison, are afraid to give them to anyone, including airport security. But leaving them for three days with the hotel guy was not scary at all, except for the Turkish prison part. If you've ever used Turkish towels, you'll know why you want to avoid that.

The hotelier was pleasant, but adamant. "You *must* have your passport. For the police." Apparently, while we strolled around Venice with our children, we could be arrested for not having passports, because if we had filled out that little form, once we committed a terrorist act, they could arrest us. I felt safer already.

We tried to look non threatening but kinda threatening; did we *have* to go all the way back to Modena?

"Do you have *anyone* in Modena who can fax a copy of your passport?" Uh, no, in Modena we had us, and we were right there. We were SO not getting the threat to international security posed by four suburbanites with rolling luggage. If Annalise *were* in possession of any intel, she would have spilled them as soon as someone asked her. "Mom, do you know what Dad is getting you for your birthday? It's a secret!! It's…" But she didn't really run in those circles.

Weirdly, Andy remembered his passport number. I am lucky if I remember the number of offspring I have produced, even when they were both chewing in my ear, in stereo. But Andy filled out the form, the hotel owner was satisfied, and I still don't know whether Andy actually knew his passport number or is the kind of guy who risks Turkish prison to avoid six extra hours on a train. I love a man of mystery.

After our Passport Adventure, it was time to go to Venice. We took a bus. It was crowded, and the children were leaning against a space reserved for luggage, when I noticed that Alex was about to step on a long thin box. It was completely covered in bubble wrap, meticulously taped, and looked like an expensive souvenir. I asked Alex to move. A young man stepped from the back of the bus to retrieve his box; oh good, he'll keep it safe. But at the next stop, when the rear door opened, he flung the carefully wrapped package into the bushes.

Game on. What just happened? Was the package flinger a drug courier, making a scheduled delivery?

Or omniscient, and knew that the package contained:

Nothing?

Plastique explosives that didn't explode on impact with bushes?

My Costco underwear, so it was okay to throw it off the bus?

I had no clue, but I smiled at Signore Flinger, hoping that at the next stop, he wouldn't toss out my backpack.

We bumped along, moving toward Venice. The bus darkened; a cloud blocked the sun. No, tenuously clinging to the window was a wasp the size of Pennsylvania. If that sucker had a saddle, we could ride it into town.

A young woman in neon pink eyeshadow and a matching fuchsia shirt was sitting next to the window, just below the beast. Her eyes widened. This was a good idea because her eyelids were the color of tropical flowers. Let's just take a moment to imagine what an insect that size would look like on someone's eye: "Aaaiiiiiieeeeee…"

Again, the package flinger moved into action. He smoothly lowered the top half of the window. But the wasp was too big to haul himself three inches, and heeey, is that an orchid? Signore Flinger gently trapped the beast in the curtain, then crushed it against the glass. The carcass hit the floor with a thump, which was hard to hear over my muffled scream.

I smiled at the flinger again, but kept a hand on my backpack.

The bus pulled into a parking lot that was growling with diesel engines. To get into Venice, you climb a canal bridge, and on your left, at the base of the bridge, is the train station. In front of the station a small crowd packed around a rock band; street musicians are common in Europe. But this was Venice, so it was no ordinary band. The group was four Native Americans encrusted with so much Day-Glo leather, feathers, and beads they extended several feet in every direction. That garb was not native, even for Vegas show-girls. They were the Liberaces of the Lakotas.

They sang what sounded like traditional Plains Indian chants, but with a Madonna-esque melody and a rollicky pop beat. Who knew that lyrics involving buffalo could be so infectious? Even their accessories were the Real McCoy: their guitar case, propped open against a plastic McDonald's sign, was tastefully draped with a fox pelt. It was more a chunk than a slice of Americana.

That little tableau was a lot to absorb, just off the bus with a canal in plain view, and it raised as many questions as the package flinger.

When career planning, how do you decide to don Native American regalia and sing Plains-Indian pop at the foot of the Venetian train station? Now that I am unemployed, it's good to know there are job options not covered in *What Color Is Your Parachute*.

No worries, I thought. I'll cross that bridge when I come to it.

So we did. We climbed a bridge, and the bridge was over the Grand Canal, which is an extremely cool bit of very dirty water. Along the canal are the marble lace buildings you've seen in photos, but you may not have noticed the laundry hanging from some of the balconies. Unlike me, Venetians had no trouble buying pants.

There were a bazillion tourists. Travelers, who are *not* tourists, always complain about tourists, who *are*.

Am not.

Most of the day-trippers wore the usual attire, jeans and spandex strained to the breaking point, but some outfits defied explanation. For example, a young lass had on a t-shirt with a bare and bulging midriff, which was literally joined at the hip to knickers that buttoned at the knee. Her knee socks were made of thick tan lace shot through with ribbon that tied at the knee and, like the shirt, clutched the knickers in a confusing embrace. To bottom it all off, the toe ends of her lace socks were swallowed up in beige suede clodhoppers. These kinds of overly complicated clothing choices dangerously interfered with my ability to process the landscape. It wasn't as much to get into my head as the Shoshone Elvises, but still, it was a challenge to take in all of those unrelated components, while trying not to fall into a canal.

The guidebooks call Venice the most expensive city in the world. When I asked the hotel guy *why* Venice was so expensive, he smiled and said, "*Venezia e unica,*" Venice is unique. That attitude only encourages the Venetians to hike up the prices, because when tourists *expect* to be gouged, they don't complain. That little phrase has been used since the first tourist guide was printed on papyrus: "Holy Moses, Venice is outrageous!" If it's written right there in Frommer's Travel Guide, you're not going to squawk. "Aaah," you'll say, when the waiter charges you 35 euros for three bottled waters. "No wonder the guidebook says…"

While waiting for takeout sandwiches from a sidewalk cafe', I watched a waiter grab three packages of pasta from a freezer. He tossed them to the cook, who ripped off the paper tops, threw the contents in the microwave, and sloshed the steaming tagliatelle onto pasta platters. For this backbreaking labor they charged almost 20 bucks, a bargain lunch in Venice.

For dinner we went to actual restaurants and had fabulous meals of pasta, pizza, seafood. But one place advertised fresh *local* seafood—dishes of fried local small fish. Is *that* a good idea? The canals are the green of antifreeze, with the neon glow dialed down a notch by a tinge of brown from sediment, or worse. Glistening on the water are chunks of floating large things, and empty water bottles. Maybe they leave the bottles floating so they can catch the little fish.

I am not going to talk about gondolas, that is so cliché, and hey, we're travelers, not tourists, so we knew from the guidebook that gondolas are insanely expensive. And most of the gondola boarding areas are on big piers off the Grand Canal, with long lines of, ya know, tourists. It's not that you think that each gondoliere just *happens* to have a long thin boat and a pole, and a burning need to show you Venice, but still, the gondola boarding process at Rialto seems a little crafty. And you'd think that prices go down at night, when you technically can't see anything, but apparently people pay a lot to make out in a gondola.

Ohhh.

So we weren't falling for any gondola nonsense. But at the end of a golden day, I saw the perfect gondoliere photo opportunity: tucked into a bend of a gilded canal was a gondoliere parked with his slim black craft. He was tall, dark, with a red striped shirt and a straw hat with a big red ribbon. His perfect torso stretched his red stripes very wide across his broad chest, and very little across his narrow abs. He was posing for the cover of *Time Magazine's* "Gondoliere of the Year"; his shoulders were huge, his hat manfully askew, and he curled around his cellphone like… oh, never mind.

I took his photo. As we walked down the steps, he gave us the gondoliere spiel. He would give us a break on the price if he could drop us off at Rialto, where he would cook for his aging mother and oil his pecs. Or at least I think he said that about his mother. When I asked, "How much," I was preconditioned by the guidebooks to expect an insanely high price, so when he said 100 euros, which was in fact an insanely high price, I thought we were getting a great deal.

So I said yes, and there we were, in a heavily enameled black boat, sunk into decadently comfy cushions. We were gliding past the former palaces of Giuseppe Verdi and Casanova, which were slipping beneath the waves from the weight of my kids' college funds. Maybe we could scoop up a few bottles of fish, for dinner. Behind us, Marco's pecs were working overtime, for his mother.

Sometimes a great deal will cost ya.

Chapter 39
Thar She Blows

In spring, we spent a few days in Tenerife, an island owned by Spain. We juggled multiple cultures: we stayed in a Spanish resort with Indonesian architecture that served fabulous Indian food, and all the tourists were British. Annalise was our designated Spanish speaker. Her only qualifications were that she took Spanish in first grade and had a *Fun with Spanish* computer game that she played in "English" mode. She kept saying "*Ola*" to people who spoke English, but at dinner she got a smile from our waitress when she said "*me gusta*" about her spaghetti.

On our first day at the beach we stopped at a souvenir hut to buy beach supplies: hats, sunglasses, and sandals. Alex closely monitored my hat purchase, vetoing one model with a shriek—"No, it's too geezer!!"—and another with a groan, "No, it's too teenager." I found one that was juuust right and was allowed to buy it.

I'd traded jeans and a black turtleneck for an Italian bathing suit and a coverup. You're welcome, Europe, for my modesty. Europe did not return the favor. We were at a beach strewn with bellies stretched by sun and sundaes, yet bikinis ruled this land.

Most men seemed to have gotten the memo: after the age of six, wear boxers. But alas, many males clung to Spandex long after Spandex should cling to them.

The women on this beach were no more discrete. Far too many bikinis have been sold to those who had no concern for the consequences. There were failures of software and hardware, a lot of sloshing and spillage, and body parts running amuck. Oh, the humanity. And then there were the *grande dames* who forsook tops completely: northern exposure in a southern climate.

Europeans think Americans are prudes. Guilty. But while the trim young mother playing catch with her son (she had quite an arm, that one) was pleasantly disconcerting, I didn't need to see acres of flab interrupted by a nipple the size of a Frisbee.

We left the beach to have lunch and fell for a place with a balcony over-looking the water. The Breeze Inn had a tiny patio with umbrellas, and a set of steps leading to apartments on upper floors. From afar, the waitresses looked like Twiggy, but it was hard to get a good look at them because they wouldn't come anywhere near our table. After they brought us drinks, further contact was prohibited. There were two waitresses, nine tables, and almost eight customers. No wonder they couldn't take our order.

Lord knows I tried. I tried to catch their eye as they passed our table, but they were absorbed with emergencies: clearing a cup. Straightening a teaspoon. Or gazing at the sea. My seat was in the sun, and the ice in my water melted and started to boil, but still I couldn't order.

A hearty German couple sat down, ordered drinks, and received food. Then a group of young women sat down to our left. Although they looked like the wait-resses, they shared our affliction: they were entitled to drinks, but nothing more.

After twenty minutes of waiting, I made a bold move: I said, *"Excuse me."* Although people on the beach far below turned in their deck chairs to see what the matter was, our server, who passed so close that I inhaled polyester fibers from her dress, didn't hear me.

Of course not. She was intent on smoothing a napkin at a neighboring table. In desperation, I attempted to excuse myself with the other waitress. But I was inexcusable.

I glanced at a pair of young lovers at the next table. They had food, they had each other, all was well. The solid young woman methodically dissected a hamburger with a knife and fork and the grim determination of an anaconda devouring a steer. Her devoted swain stroked her arm tenderly—what a brave man; I would have been afraid to interrupt her at her feed.

A younger German couple sat down, waited expectantly, and was sadly disappointed; apparently neither youth nor German heritage ensured service.

Alex swatted at a bug and won. It lay on the floor between the tables. The newly arrived German man asked, "Mosquito?"

I wanted to answer, "Honey, it's fresh, and it's dead. Better eat that while you have a chance, because nothing else is coming." But I couldn't say that in German.

The abandoned young women developed hostile stares. The newly arrived Germans developed bulging discs in their necks from constantly swiv-eling to stare at the waitresses.

Bored, I watched people descend the stairs from the upper floors. A series of Adonises appeared. Trim, tan, muscled. They carried volleyballs. Or towels. Or volleyballs. They were mesmerizing, and the distraction carried me through the next stage of hunger: drooling. Or maybe the drooling was all about the Adonises.

The determined lass polished off her burger. The sight of her empty plate, or maybe her dormant knife, triggered in her lover an uncontrollable desire. He held her face in his hands. He cupped her chin in his fingers. He pulled her closer and then…

"OH MY GOD!!! OH MY GOD!!!" Let's just say what happened next was disgusting. If you'd like to hold on to your next several meals, skip the next sentence.

Well here you are, and it's your own darn fault: He… no, I can't say it.

He… let's just say that he relieved her pores of certain facial impurities. At the table.

OH MY GOOOODDDDDD!!!

We were finally served, although by that time, I was no longer interested in eating.

And then I understood. Maybe the lovers were regulars. Every day they ordered lunch, she ate her hamburger, pop went the weasel, and everyone in the restaurant got "seesick." What was the point of serving people who had lost all their desire for food? The Twiggies were trapped in a Sisyphean struggle, and they had dropped the ball.

Thar she blows, indeed. And you thought I meant the bikinis.

Chapter 40
Flight Risk

The delightful thing about living in Europe is that so much cool stuff is so tantalizingly close, and getting there is half the fun, but only if you have a private jet or a first-class seat on a bullet train. In our year in Italy, we traveled by low-cost airline or by second-class train. Each trip was fascinating, and because I was traveling with my family, often painfully funny.

Several times, we flew to London. Once you're in Europe, you can do that sort of thing. You can fly to London like it's a trip to the deli. A super far away deli that requires a plane, and passports, and luggage. But hey, I didn't say it was easy. No really, that was you.

Because flying is not all that easy, really. First you have to find the suitcases, which all have developed broken zippers and gaping holes in the sides, and blame must be assigned for the damage:

"*You're* the one who insisted on taking *five* pairs of underwear!!"

"For *five days*!!"

That led into sub-fights about who was taking so much that the zippers were blowing out, and who was taking so little there were public health implications. People who travel while married should never do so in front of the children.

I finished packing. And then I learned that because we were flying on a low-cost airline, we were under a baggage restriction. Laid end to end, the total dimensions of the contents of our luggage could not exceed 27.5 centimeters. Anything over the limit cost 25 euros per centimeter, per minute. I had no idea how to comply with that requirement, so I got a look in my eye that tells Andy to continue this conversation would lead to emotional, and perhaps physical, scarring. He wisely dropped it and tucked two extra credit cards into his wallet.

Before we left the apartment, I tried to clean up enough so while we were gone, our lifestyle choices wouldn't horrify Giovanna and/or attract a family of crazed wolverines. We were running out of time, so I asked Alex, who had been unable to locate his shoes but was intent on a game of *Guitar Hero* to... NOOOO—sweep the floor. He shrieked in shock: he was pained, he was in agony, he was about to get a free trip to London, and he'd better be holding a broom ASAP, or he'd be flossing with it. Annalise had to be gently reminded, for the 40th time, to:

"GO. FIND. YOUR. SHOES... NOOOOOWWWWWW!!"

When my blood pressure had risen sufficiently to make me levitate, she finally did it.

A spoon full of sugar?! I don't *think* so. Let's consider: in Mary Poppins, did the children decide to tidy up the nursery because the nanny was singing, or because she gave them multicolored pharmaceuticals?

With a little more yelling, and some threats, the nursery was spit-spot and we could catch the bus to the airport. The bus to the airport was cheap, and very convenient if you survived getting in and out of the bus. The forward door was fine. But if you walked to the back of the bus, on the left, cleverly concealed to ensure that you didn't notice, were jagged steel steps that plummeted 20 feet straight down. The steps ended at an exit door; the door opened with a heavy horizontal bar that jutted out at a murderous angle.

The exit bar was a well-designed safety feature. It ensured that before you accordion-pleated your vertebrae by landing headfirst on the bottom step, you'd comfortably lose consciousness by clocking yourself on the exit bar on the way down. Apparently Italian trial lawyers never take a bus to the airport, or they are all killed when they don't see the steps.

Along the highway to the Bologna airport, we passed miles of farm fields: rich brown soil tilled and sown, with a thin white plume of smoke every few acres. The smoke may have been the result of a traditional farming technique, but I suspected that the plume had a more nefarious source. The smoke was actually created by Italian postal workers when they burned certified copies of the blank pages of American passports. While no one *needs* the blank ones, the fine ash is exceptionally good for the soil. That's why Italian produce tastes so good; I liked knowing that with every document I submitted to the Italian government, I was doing my part to improve the taste of plum tomatoes.

At the airport, we had to go through security. Even after 9-11, Europeans didn't catch on that the greatest risk to an airplane came from weaponry concealed in size seven ballerina flats. So, to satisfy European security, I could keep my shoes on, but all jackets had to come off. I wore every jacket I owned, to leave room in the suitcase for Andy's socks, so removing and replacing my outerwear took several hours.

While I reassembled my wardrobe, I had time for a quick score check in the War on Terror. I didn't know who won in the European Division. Was it the terrorists, because Europeans had to take off their jackets? Or the Europeans, because they won the part about keeping on their shoes? It's possible that the tiebreaker was my Schwarzkopf conditioner.

I have faith in Italian airport security. During our prior sabbatical, Alex had potentially fatal food allergies, so I took six EpiPen syringes in my carry-on luggage. When that bag went through the X-ray machine, the Italians saw the syringes and opened the boxes. The slim lines could have been six knives lying on their sides, and besides, I was wearing those dangerous shoes. I was grateful that Italian security wanted to see what was in the boxes. When I took that same bag through Germany, those inspectors assumed that sullen scowls sufficiently deterred terrorism, and they didn't consider six rapier-thin pieces of metal worth a look-see. I think the Germans *did* win that round in the War on Terror. They weren't terrified, they weren't even interested.

After we cleared security, we had to stop at the immigration desk and show our passports. In this phase, steely eyed skeptics scrutinized our documents. This always makes me paranoid; I must have done *something* to deserve that look, so I always want to blurt out a pre-emptive confession. "Alright—Yesss—I AM a Soviet... spppyy!!!" Such a confession would not be particularly helpful to the immigration authorities because technically, the Soviets are Russians again, and no, I'm not a spy, I can't even work my phone's camera. But if they were getting paid to make me nervous, I wanted to get my money's worth.

I was a bit peevish because the whole *point* of passing through immigration was to get a cool stamp on my passport. In most countries, immigration officials gave you a cool little stamp when you entered, and a different one when you left. So, when the trip was over and you were sitting at your molded plastic desk in a bleak office cubicle, you could fan yourself with your passport and languidly review the little odd symbols for each nation you visited, murmuring softly—but not *so* softly that no one could hear you—"*Aaaah, Tangiers.*" If you couldn't be a spy, at least you could mope for an interesting reason.

But NO, you're not going to get any more cool little stamps, because the Europeans took all the fun out of crossing their borders.

When they created the European Union, which is a group of countries that get to sneer at Americans for lots of perfectly valid reasons, the spoilsport EU nations decided that everyone could travel between EU countries without having to get cool symbols stamped on their passports. It was a huge cost cutting measure; they saved enough money on those little ink pads to fund socialized medicine.[23]

And the elimination of passport stamping ensured the success of Italian agriculture. No matter how many times you traveled in Europe, all of the pages of your passport would remain blank, but thanks to Italian bureaucracy, you'd have to copy the blank pages anyway, because burning the useless copies is good for the soil.

It's that kind of one-worldish cooperation among nations that gives Republicans the heebie jeebies, and rightly so. Or maybe they're disturbed because the Europeans called it a Union, and then, you know, there's the whole socialized medicine thing.

Travel is exhausting. I went through all that and I hadn't even reached the plane.

I'm going to have to ask for an apology for your deli metaphor; you were totally wrong about that.

---

23   Brexit made all that passport stuff way more confusing, but Italians will still require the copying of blank pages of passports, because... tomatoes.

Chapter 41
UFLR Air—How to Make Enemies Without Even Trying

We settled into our seats on Unidentified for Legal Reasons (UFLR) Air, a low-cost European airline. We boarded the plane in our usual way, which involved making our fellow passengers homicidal.

The boarding process at UFLR Air was a cross between a stampede and a game of musical chairs; not even the pilot got an assigned seat.

When we reached the departure gate, the kids and I took our places in the clump of humanity that constitutes an Italian line while Andy made his way to the front of the pack. He called this "boarding the plane" but I called this "trying to get us killed at the airport." He always reached the gate attendant several minutes before we did, and because Andy held the tickets and passports for all four of us, the attendant was forced to retrieve us from the back of the line.

Unlike Andy, I am the same height as an Italian, so on our way to the front, I looked directly into the outraged eyes of the many people we passed. I pretended that was why they are called "passengers."

Once in my seat, I tried to recover from the trauma of our trip through security. No matter how many flights my kids took, or how many hours we waited in a security line, when we reached the security conveyor belt, my offspring were shocked to learn that they had to empty their pockets and put their carry-on bags onto the belt so the bags could be x-rayed.

Shocked, I say.

With 4,000 frazzled travelers behind us, Annalise insisted on placing onto the belt random pieces of clothing and body parts in compliance with security regulations of her own making, while Alex devoted his entire attention to a detailed explanation of an obscure computer game.

In a desperate attempt to keep the line moving, I grabbed an empty bin and slammed it down in front of my son, hoping to interrupt his soliloquy on the philosophical underpinnings of *Prince of Persia*. Before I could stop him, he would take up his usual position just before the entrance to the baggage x-ray machine, where he would pause to contemplate an unspecified spot in space.

After a frantic bark from his irrationally harried mother, he would reach into the 700 pockets of his cargo shorts, and slooowwwly extricate 527 bits of effluvia, which he arranged, alphabetically, in the plastic bin. He was carrying enough metal to stock a foundry—where did he *get* all this stuff? And why did he carry it around?

Meanwhile, Andy was busy disassembling his computer and creating his own Metalhenge, which left me plenty of time to notice that we were backing up the security line for several hundred miles. All four of our carry-ons littered the floor behind us, so I frantically piled our bags onto the belt. But I couldn't move the bags forward because Alex was blocking the entrance to the x-ray machine, and he still had 300 pockets to empty. So our luggage, Annalise's extraneous contributions, and Alex's overflowing container would take up the entire conveyor belt.

Despite my explanatory pantomime, no one seemed to grasp that all of those things could, with just a little effort, slide forward so that other people could put *their* stuff onto the belt.

When I was finally able to clear the family logjam at the entrance to the x-ray machine, we repeated the same process in reverse on the other side, which took even longer, and caused my blood pressure to triple. On a positive note, hyperventilation ensured that in case of a loss of cabin pressure, I wouldn't need oxygen.

There should be an early boarding option for people with a dangerous medical condition, like traveling with my family.

Once we had walked to our seats and adjusted our seat belts, we'd enjoyed all of the amenities available on this flight. Free beverage service? A small bottle of water cost six euros—about $8.50 USD—and if this airline could find a way, it would charge you for your own spit.

To keep prices low, UFLR Air imposed incomprehensible weight restrictions. Each checked bag had to weigh less than 15 kilos, or the square root of 27.3 hectares. Even carry-ons were limited to ten kilos, or 14 degrees Celsius. Because the airline could charge $70 extra for a bag an ounce over the weight limit, UFLR Air baggage inspectors lay in wait in every nook and cranny of the airport, including in the stalls of the restrooms, in the hopes that humidity or the purchase of a pack of gum increased the weight of a bag enough to trigger the fee.

When we flew to Bari, we were close to the weight limit on all our bags, which meant we couldn't shop without fear of baggage fees on the return flight. So I couldn't buy anything in Bari, except for a small jar of broccoli in olive oil. And a ceramic plate. Okay, and also a large bottle of limoncello, but no one has ever sipped limoncello and thought, "Baggage restriction." True, yes, there was also a set of framed photographs of the *trulli* in Alberobello, but those photographs weighed a lot less than the buildings they depicted, and where were the baggage inspectors when I was buying the plate?

I suspect that I had a passive aggressive response to the UFLR weight restrictions, but don't tell Andy, because he thinks I'm just crazy.

Although weight restrictions on low-cost airlines mean that passengers are not allowed to bring aboard nonessentials like insulin and heart medication, even UFLR flights included a duty-free cart, which sells alcohol and perfume. Duty free carts on airplanes have always puzzled me—does the fear of dying in a plane crash make buying overpriced Scotch and a liter of Chanel No. 5 seem like a reasonable thing to do? And why do airlines sell just *those* items? Why not offer something useful, like craft kits?

> *Welcome aboard! As a service to our passengers, our flight attendants are now coming through the aisles with all the supplies you'll need to construct your own combination neck pillow/passport holder/airsickness bag!*

On UFLR Air, you never had to remove the emergency information card from the pocket of the seat back in front of you, because there *was* no pocket on the seat back in front of you. The safety information was printed directly on the seat back, which was conveniently located just beyond my eyelashes.

Since I didn't have to occupy myself with eating snacks or drinking anything but my own saliva, I studied the safety information sticker. A series of cartoons provided helpful information, such as what I wouldn't be allowed to take with me if the plane crashed any harder than it did on a regular landing.

Based on the drawings, if the plane crashed, I should leave behind my glasses. If I took off my glasses, I wouldn't know whether the plane had actually crashed, so that would help prevent me from panicking. And without my glasses I would be so blind I wouldn't be able to leave my seat; that would also cut down on crowding in the aisles that would delay the safe evacuation of the other passengers.

Another cartoon indicated that I must leave behind my high-heeled shoes, but since I would die in my seat wearing my terrorist flats, I ignored that.

A third drawing was puzzling. If the plane crashed, I wouldn't be allowed to exit the plane with what appeared to be an angry clam and some oddly shaped linguine. Perhaps UFLR Air was trying to prevent a safety crisis caused by passengers fleeing with spaghetti in spicy clam sauce.

There were also a series of drawings about how to use my life jacket in the event of a water landing. Water landings required no restrictions on pasta with clam sauce, so I prefer to crash into water, if anyone wants to know.

Now that I knew all about my plane crash options, I could relax and enjoy the rest of the flight to Pisa. At least until we had to get off the plane and had to get on an escalator. If I reached the escalator before anyone in my family, I could escalate as safely as a UFLR passenger without glasses, or stilettos, or *Penne Vongole Arrabbiata*.

But if I were behind Andy or the kids, I knew that when they got off the escalator, they would stand at the bottom of that moving walkway, put down all of their luggage, and come to a complete standstill just beyond the last steel-jawed step. When the escalator spit me off, I would be propelled, flailing, into the wall o' luggage that protected my family members, who would wait until the last possible nanosecond to move out of the way. My desperate attempts to avoid a collision amused all the passengers we antagonized while boarding and in the security line, so we lived to take another flight.

Travel is so relaxing. I wonder if I can buy a case of limoncello in Pisa?

Chapter 42
Signs

One of the few times we rented a car in Europe, Andy found a way to accelerate my travel worries, and not just because we were in the UK and driving "on the wrong side of the road." You would think that Andy would have forgotten that one time, *one time*, in Australia when he pulled into traffic, and I screamed: "YOU'RE GOING THE WRONG WAAAAAAY!" That one time, my hysterical howl was not particularly helpful, because he *was* going the right way, for Australia. Inexplicably, Andy decided not to trust my navigational skills for the rest of our lives. But in England, he developed a bizarre foot affliction that challenged my voicebox even more than usual.

After Pisa, we took a 16-day road trip in the UK. We started with a visit to friends in Hull, in Northern England. To get there, we rented a car and drove two-and-a-half hours, entirely on the wrong side of the road. After a while, you get used to it, especially if you keep your hands over eyes and mouth. If you drove for two hours on the wrong side of the road in the US, I wonder if you'd get used to that, too.

On the way to Hull, I remembered why I hadn't driven with Andy in seven months. *Besides* that we didn't have a car in Italy. Andy believed that changing lanes required him to ignite the rear license plate of the car in front of us. He would get so close that our license plates set off sparks. Only when he saw an actual flame leaping over the hood would he lurch the wheel and careen into the next lane. On a day with a lot of lane changes, the kids could roast an entire pack of marshmallows on the front grill of our car.

I was perfectly comfortable with this level of terror when my sweetie upped the ante. On the drive to Hull, between lane changes, Andy would suddenly stomp on the gas pedal, thrash his legs, and bellow in pain. We'd surge forward into whatever direction the flailing led us, and when my shrieking stopped, I learned that he had a leg cramp.

Andy gets cramps only when he's driving. We can sit on the couch, chatting quietly, and out of nowhere, nothing happens: his leg is fine. In the low hum of a restaurant, just when I least expect it, he's as still as a country pond. But in a speeding car, with vehicles on all sides of us driving in the wrong direction, he was yelping and stomping the gas pedal like Jed Clampett at a hoedown. I love a relationship full of surprises.

I reached Hull with my vocal cords hanging in shreds. The next morning for brekkie, we had English muffins. This disturbed me. Brits have given perfectly innocuous items perfectly adorable names: sausage and mashed potatoes are "Bangers and Mash," leftover vegetables are "Bubbles and Squeak." But for some reason, no one bothered to come up with a good name for toaster muffins. It's not as if the United Kingdom didn't have good writers handy, what with Shakespeare and Dickens and a pack of Bronte sisters. But when they got around to naming muffins, Brits put in no effort at all. With all the credit they get for literary excellence, they should get a few demerits for that.

We left our friends to drive to Wales. It was the height of summer, so of course it was cold and raining. In Wales, August is just another opportunity to wear thick wet fleece, but in flirty tropical colors.

Along the way we stopped at Shakespeare's birthplace, and Stonehenge. In Liverpool we spent hours in a museum dedicated to the Beatles. Fab, those four. Then we drove to Leeds, where the weather forecaster described the day's cumulonimbus activity in colors ranging from white to black. "Light gray clouds in the morning, followed by dark gray clouds in the afternoon. Tomorrow, rain." British landfills must be full of the cheery sun magnets once sold to television meteorologists all over the world.

Despite the weather in the UK, it was a relief to be in a place where I could read all of the signs, although most of the time I didn't know what they meant. In the hallway of our British hotel, a glass door was etched with the words: "Only for emergency evacuations. Not for hotel guests." I guess we'd have to fend for ourselves, then. Other signs said, "This door is alarmed." "This fire extinguisher is alarmed." I was getting a little alarmed, too.

Many of the clothing stores had "Sale!" signs in their windows, with the usual well-togged mannequins. But most of the shops also displayed a placard that said, "Sale continues inside." What was *that* about? Did Brits assume that the sale applied only to the items in the window? Where *else* would the sale be held, if not inside the store?

Signs are dangerous only if they advertise savings of up to 70 percent off. But when you're driving on the wrong side of the road, clarity saves lives. The most frequently used British highway sign was "Give Way." I found this confusing. Give way on what, exactly? Socialized medicine? Pointless spelling differences? (Okay, I'll give way on theatre, they do have Shakespeare. But Colour? Centre? No, I'm not yielding on those).

"Give Way" was the most straightforward of the bunch. What on earth did they mean by "Discontinuous Emergency Refuge for Two Miles?" "Que After JCT?" "Works Unit Only?" No wonder British drivers all started going the wrong way—they were trying to escape the highway department.

In Wales, road signs are printed in Welsh and English. Although British English can be mystifying, Welsh sounds like a spoon caught in a garbage disposal, and looks like a game of drunken Scrabble. For example, *Yr Wyddgrug Moldnear* is an actual town, and so is *Llanfairpwllgwyngyllgogerychwyrndrobwllllantysiliogogogoch.* [24]

Welsh warning signs are shaped like tall triangles, with a large exclamation point at the peak, and the reason for alarm in the middle. Roadside signs warned us to be on the alert for *daerafochen,* bilingual badgers. I wondered what that was all about. Would we be waylaid by annoyingly persistent rodents? How would that play out? *"Saaay, are you going to eat that yyllwwsyws?"* I suppose a polite refusal wouldn't suffice, because they're, you know, badgers.

There was an app that translated Welsh road signs; it's since been taken down. But it wouldn't have helped guard against actual Welsh road hazards; the app's dictionary had no word for "badger."

We spent the rest of that trip on the Cote d'Azur in the south of France, where we visited my mom's cousin Clare at her villa.[25] Clare's mother and my grandmother were sisters, and together we explored our family history. Propped on chaise lounges on her breezy tiled patio, we mapped our shared genes in a handwritten scrawl that sprawled across a notebook page like fan coral. For every name, there was a story, some of

24   The name means: "St Mary's Church in the Hollow of the White Hazel near a Rapid Whirlpool and the Church of St. Tysilio near the Red Cave."
25   Chatting with Clare and Eric and my incredible English cousins at dinner, I loved that while this family lived a world away, they made us feel at home.

them tragic: my aunt developed scleroderma, my cousin died at 40. Clare's sister lost one young husband to cancer, and then a second to war. Clare answered the door when that dreaded telegram came. How do you tell your sister, who has two small sons, that she is a widow? For the second time?

Clare went to grad school at Stanford, where she met and married a man who was knighted. They live in London, surrounded by their five beautiful and brilliant daughters and a flock of fascinating grandchildren. Clare was a young wife in the 1950s, an American who married a Brit and never looked back. Her road *was* revolutionary. The hours we spent over that notebook are some of my most precious memories of that year.

Uh oh. My little pretties, the sand in the hourglass was running down, and a big bucket of cold water was about to be sloshed all over my cackling persona. Work? I couldn't go back to *wooork*. Things were going so well in Italy, what with the cappuccino, and the gelato, and the infinitely fascinating forms of pasta and Italian shoe design. With only four more months left on my ruby slippers, I wasn't ready to turn them in for work boots.

When we got back to Modena, I could read the signs, and they all said: *"It's almost time to go home."*

That was a warning I *could* understand.

Chapter 43
Keeping Track

Travelling in Europe we sometimes flew, and rented a car or two, but most of the time we traveled by train, which is relaxing as long as you don't do it with my family. To celebrate Annalise's birthday, we spent a week and a small fortune in Paris. We knew it was her birthday because she reminded us every 27 seconds: "Did you know it's my birthday?" As her parents, we were relatively familiar with the date of her birth; she tried so hard to jump the gun on her arrival, I had to take anti-contraction medication. Although she was born in the wee hours of April 11, Annalise counted as her birth date all of the false starts and premature labor. So for her, the festivities started in mid-March. There's no better way to celebrate parental sleep loss than an overnight train trip to Paris.

Packing for trains is easy: you can't take anything. Whatever you pack must be hurtled down a million steps beneath the station, then hauled back up to the platform, all of which involves a lot of unsightly gasping, and tucking all of your pulled muscles back into your clothing.

Once you have hoisted yourself onto an Italian train platform, the only air space free of secondhand smoke is found on the tracks, in the area between the engine and the first car. While hiding under the train is discouraged, waiting on a platform crowded with every smoker in Italy means that with every breath, you can hear your lung cells seize up and die. While trying to breathe through your tear ducts, you vow that your obituary will list your cause of death as mass murder, by train.

But surviving the wait on the platform is only the first of many challenges. When the train arrives, you have to get on it. When the train pulls in, five million people have to get off, and seven million people have to get on. Somewhere in that crowd is you and your luggage, your spouse and his luggage, and your children and whatever luggage they didn't leave in the station. And all of those people are trying to squeeze through a space the size of a train door.

European train doors are at best two feet wide and are designed to stick half-way closed; if you're an optimist, halfway open. The doors are perched at the top of steep steel steps, and the lowest rung is at least 18 inches above the ground. Everyone and everything must get on and off that step within three minutes of the train's arrival, or you're stuck for another round of Platform Smoke Roulette.

When the train arrives, you stand in front of the door as people fling themselves and their suitcases off the high step. They aim for a soft landing, preferably on someone's thigh. De-training alone takes several minutes, so, with seconds to go before the train pulls out, you must heave your child and her suitcase stuffed with commemorative rocks onto the top step. She comes to a dead stop in the doorway, to reflect on the excitement of travel, or to read a book, and as the train picks up speed you hurl yourself, and the packet of Kleenex you will fashion into a travel wardrobe, onto the train.

Then you find a seat. For one person, this is no problem. For four people, one of whom (Annalise) insists on sitting on the south-facing seat on a westward train, and an east-facing seat on any train whose destination ends in a vowel, getting seated can be tricky. If the pickiness in seating continues, you look for the most menacing person in the compartment to ask whether he has ever considered starting a business which employs seven-year-old chimney sweeps. Travel is so broadening when it exposes children to new career options.

For the trip to Paris, we booked a *couchette*. Couchette is French for sleeper car, but the term means "if you plan to sleep in here you are woefully delusional." Our first task was to locate the correct car. Our couchette was in Car 97, which you might believe was located between cars 96 and 98. But not on this train. On this train, which had about 100 cars, the 70s were in the same general location, the 80s mixed and matched, but the 90s were alll over the map.

Because we would be gone for a week and a half, we took Big Red, a beast of a suitcase, and three smaller ones. As the train roared into the station, Andy watched Car 97 roll by and tried to board there. "NOOO!" shouted the conductor.

"But that's Car 97," said Andy.

"No, it isn't," said the conductor, "that's at the other end of the train."

Trying to find a single car out of 100 is not easy from outside a train, especially one that is leaving. So we boarded, to find it from the inside. But that meant heaving luggage, including Big Red, through the clogged and narrow corridors of a moving train, which is a lot like navigating the intestinal passage of a constipated pterodactyl. So Andy stayed with the luggage, and the kids and I set out to find Car 97.

We boarded in the middle, and Andy saw Car 97 at the front, so we headed that way. The cars were choked with people and travel gear of every description: sagging suitcases, bloated backpacks, lemur-carrying devices. Although every passenger had a seat, and every seat had overhead storage, to facilitate movement through the lurching train, every passenger heaped all their gear in the corridor, wedged themselves diagonally across the hallway, and stood there.

This was not helpful. A woman and two children, at the tattered hour of 11 p.m., are not walking the halls for their own amusement. If you are blocking the passage, and one woman and two children are standing beside you, it's not because they have gotten on the train for the express purpose of keeping you company in the hallway.

No, really, it's not.

One man, his voluminous back an uninterrupted block of bovine obliviousness, clogged the narrow passage like a chunk of cholesterol in an artery.

"Excuse me," I said.

Nada.

"Excuse Me."

 "EXCUSE. ME."

"EXXXXCUUUUUUUSSSSSSEEEEE MEEEEEEEEEE."

Unable to bear the irritating din far below his hair-spurting ears, he reluctantly moved aside.

High school students, eyes fearful with unfamiliar freedom, also obstructed the hallway, but they recognized the crazed look of a tired mom and got out of the way before the yelling starting.

Walking through the cars was an obstacle course, but getting between them was like riding the Moving Walkway from Hell. The doors between the cars sealed as tightly as Tupperware lids and opened only with a wrenching jerk, or sometimes a jerky wench, depending on the train. On the floor of the vestibule where the cars connected there were metal plates that bucked and jolted, and on each side of the coupling there was a gap large enough for a child to fall in up to her thigh. Through the holes in the joining plates, I could see the tracks rushing by below. But since the lurching of the train kept Annalise airborne most of the time she was in a vestibule, unlike a London hotel door, I was not alarmed.

We headed for the front, where Andy said he saw Car 97. We ripped open door after door, plunged through the cars numbered in the 60s, the 70s, the 80s, the 90s… aaah, Car 96. 97 must be next! But no: at the front of Car 96, there was a window, through which we saw the back of the engine. Car 97, where are you???

We turned back. I found a porter and asked for 97. He shrugged philosophically; he had no idea, and no interest in finding out. It was 11:30. I had two kids and no place to sleep. My family insanity genes activated, and I morphed into a raging lunatic. "WHERE IS IT? WHY DON'T YOU KNOW WHERE THE CAR IS?? IT'S *YOUR* TRAIN!!"

This had no effect. *Niente.* Apparently train porters are impervious to people screaming at them, and besides, only half my genes are Italian.

We stayed on track. We passed Andy, who straddled the luggage. "It's at the front, I saw it!" he insisted. But the three of us, who had been in every car in that direction, were prepared to accept that he had imagined the whole thing. It happens. We found more porters, who cheerfully confirmed that the car was at the front of the train.

This was becoming way too much like the 70s movie *The Poseidon Adventure*, and I was Shelley Winters, insanely insisting that to escape the sinking ship we had to head down, towards the hull. We kept moving, through the 50s, the 40s, now reaching the end of the train… and Car 97. Why didn't *I* think to put Car 97 between Car 46 and 49? This is exactly the kind of thing that makes me skeptical of engineers of every stripe. Because here's a disturbing Train Fact: the carriage car numbers were not enameled onto the walls, or carved in steel, they were MADE OF PAPER, and stuck on with TAPE!!! Smarmy transport planners, *here's* some training for you: if you're just going to use paper signs to identify the cars, when you *add* a car, you could easily retape the numbers, so the cars stay in order; that would be *just* the ticket.

We plunged back through 40 cars, found Andy (who continued to mumble that he saw 97 at the front, but we patted him gently and moved him along), and finally, after midnight, we got into our *couchette*.

Our sleeping compartment had six seats that theoretically turned into six cots, but only if you believe that a bed should have the dimensions of a cigarette lighter. To reach the upper cots, there was an iron ladder. The ladder connected to the iron railing of the bunk by a clever hook that was really more like a flat piece of metal. If you tilted the ladder even slightly, the heavy ladder toppled backwards, so it was highly likely that a small child, who insisted on climbing up and down 3,000 times, would detach the ladder and be flung onto the steel wall of the opposite side. Train travel is so exciting, when you're not sure about insurance.

The *couchette* was stocked with dollhouse bedding: each bunk held a single-molecule pillow, an elfin sleeve that served as both a top and bottom sheet, and a blanket. The blanket was the size of a playing card, and its loose weave siphoned heat from the body and sent it out into the cool night air. Apparently, there *was* a heater in the couchette, but a certain person with red curly hair, who was sleeping on the top bunk and was named Alexander Robert Babb Goetz, decided that it was *too hot* in the top compartment and *turned the heat off*. In the morning, a certain devoted mother, who had spent 17 grueling hours in labor to produce a red-haired person with two middle names, learned that heat was available but cruelly withheld. Over *petit dejeuner* in the dining car, the conversation turned to military school and orphanages, and stayed there for the next several days.

Not that sleep was possible, even if there was heat. When you're seated in a train, the car gently sloshes over the tracks, bobbing and weaving; riding a train is a relatively tranquil experience. That is, until another train passes on the tracks just on the other side of the window, filling the glass with a heart-stopping million tons of thrashing steel and pulsating light that hurtles within inches of your face. But in that lull in between, it's relaxing.

Lying down in a metal train compartment on a paper-thin mattress the width of a matchstick is like trying to sleep in a blender set on "puree." Between the noise and the shaking and the lack of heat (ALEX!!!), I felt like a human margarita.

Theoretically the tracks are flat and relatively straight. But every time I started to fall asleep, my brain interpreted the incessant jostling in the cold and dark as an excursion on an Antarctic rollercoaster. This was not restful. All night long, every time I drifted off, the train pitched and bucked, climbed frozen waterfalls, plummeted into frigid chasms, and slid off ice floes. Of course, if my brain cells hadn't frozen upon contact with my skull (ALEX!!!) I may have been able to convince my synapses of their safety. Between the cold (ALEX!!!) and the pureeing, my overnight trip did not include sleeping, which should have allowed me to deduct the *"couche"* from the price of the ticket.

The kids slept like, well, kids. In the morning they were thrilled they had slept on the train, because they had actually *slept* on the train. We took two more overnight train trips, to Poland and to Legoland Denmark. The experience was a lot like the third week with a newborn: loud, smelly, and, except for the staggering fatigue, mercifully hard to recall. If you're looking for an unforgettable experience to share with your kids, book an overnight train and have fun with it. If you're looking for a relaxing way to travel, fly to a really nice hotel, put the kids on an overnight train, and meet them in Paris.

Chapter 44
Paris Scenes

What is there to love about Paris? Everything, especially the cafés. There are two excellent reasons to hang out in a Paris café. One of them is *café crème*, which tastes like cappuccino but comes in a bigger cup and offers more caffeine. The other is that a café is your seat for the epic romance unfolding every moment on Paris streets.

Paris is the City of Lovers. In Paris you hear this about once every seven minutes. But technically it's the City of High Maintenance Extroverts. Parisian love, even Parisian *like*, is dramatic and public. There are continual confrontations between former flames, seething *innamorati*, and people who don't even know each other but just feel like making a scene. That's the whole point of Paris cafés: find a table facing the street, order a drink, and wait for the show to begin.

It happens everywhere. While waiting for our clothes to wash, we took our seats at a nondescript sidewalk café. Within minutes, a motorcycle blazed up and discharged a slim and lovely lass in complicated cotton and a handsome man in jeans and a suavely French sweater. They parted. He walked away slowly. The street was ordinary: a sidewalk, some small shops, some tiny cars.

A moment later the young lady had claimed the middle of the road as the center stage for her very personal drama. With a toss of her hair and a flailing of long limbs, Mademoiselle Dramatique launched into an interpretive dance on the thrilling theme, "He is a Beast, and I Will Kill Him!!" Her scarves flew, her tassels fluttered, and he had to choose between two kinds of hell: leaving, or staying.

He turned and walked into the flames of her fury.

Monsieur Gallant took her arm and gently moved the wreckage of his relationship onto the sidewalk. He soothed her frayed nerves and flying fabric with his manly devotion and a torso clad in fabulous cashmere in a subtle shade of pumpkin. She calmed, and they settled into a dreamy, swaying embrace. This segued into kissing, which conveniently reheated my coffee. Yes, yes, *now* he understood about putting the cap on the toothpaste.

Mais non, Mademoiselle Dramatique erupted anew over some fresh and searing insult. She now revealed, in lurid detail, particularly vulgar aspects of his personality and grooming habits. Oooh, TMI on his unnaturally abundant nasal hair.

Under this new barrage, Gallant's love-soaked soul was pierced and bled, audibly. He threw out his arms, threw back his head, and swallowed the sky to express the utter futility of love, and to demonstrate how sparks of sunlight lit up his impressively white teeth.

And then he was gone. Their love was broken, smashed. Little bits of it floated down and landed, like sad ashes, on my croissant. She stood in the street, screaming after him. He was a cad, her soul was shattered, and she was finished with love. As she drew into herself to experience this grief, my eye caught a familiar large red suitcase bumping along the street; I wondered if the woman rolling it had absconded with our laundry.

But Parisian love does not leave you time to think about the theft of your clothing. The young lady, who had experienced a tragic loss only moments ago, allowed her broken heart to beat almost twice before she found new romance. Or perhaps it was old romance, it was hard to tell.

In the moment I was distracted by the suitcase, Mademoiselle Dramatique was well into the business end of a honeymoon with a new beau. He may have been a former lover who happened to be walking by at the precise moment she was free. Or *this* was the soul mate for whom she had been waiting for her whole life, or for at least four and a half seconds.

Either way, they were locked in an embrace that melted the butter in my croissant; it's so refreshing that nothing ever gets cold at a sidewalk café. And then he was gone, and she was gone, and so was my café crème. They do that on purpose; it's all over in the time it takes to drink a cup of coffee.

In Paris, the complications of love are on constant display. While waiting in line at the Eiffel Tower, I overhead two men exchanging small talk.

"Are you married?" asked the older man.

"Yes," answered the young man, who was drop-dead gorgeous.

"Is your wife here?"

"No, she's at home. Once a year we each take a week's vacation, alone."

"Then who is that young lady with you?"

"She's just someone who loves to take pictures of shoes."

Now *that's* a euphemism you don't hear every day. I turned around. She was exquisitely French, thin with narrow bones and perfect skin. She had a camera in one hand, and had affixed herself to the side of his body like an octopus to the wall of an acquarium.

No question, that week she got some good shots of a heel.

In Paris, love is everywhere. On a tourist boat on the Seine, the young couple in front of us was smitten and sharing it. They sang along with the French songs on the audio tour, chuckled at their own cheesiness, and got everyone laughing with them.

They were in love in the way that makes you believe that mutual adoration, and looking fabulous in tight white pants, is all you need to be happy.

At the end of the ride, our boat docked at a pier next to a glass-walled restaurant. Behind the glass was an older couple dressed for the 19th century. His full beard overflowed his brown wool suit, vest, and creamy linen shirt. His high boots were iron-thick leather. His wife looked like a *National Geographic* photograph of an Andalusian—her dark and braided hair was bound up in a red wool beaded scarf, and a flowing white tunic encased her ample body like upholstery.

The lovers were young men. As the boat docked, the older fellow saluted them with a deeply respectful bow. He was dressed so out of his time that seeing him move was like watching an antique photo come to life. He smiled at the lovers and bowed again. The three men were delightful. The lovers were funny and warm and friendly, and as we approached a pier, they sailed into the heart of a gentleman from another century.

That's the kind of thing that makes you think people *will* be all right, after all.

And then I looked at the wife's face; it had hardened into stone. As I looked at her, I wondered if she had ever taken photographs of shoes.

Chapter 45

Hotel St. S.: You Can Czech Out Any Time You Like, But You Can Never Leave

Because I'm old and have travelled a lot, I've stayed in hundreds of hotels. I can't remember most of them, but the Hotel St. S. still makes my family laugh.

The opening line of *Anna Karenina* ("All happy families are alike; every unhappy family is unhappy in its own way") also applies to hotels. In decades of travel, I remember few "nice" hotels. But the truly wretched ones are etched into my memory like roach trails on wet soap.

Hotel K. in Amsterdam was the most spectacularly awful place I have ever tried to sleep. The walls audibly teemed with biota; I heard chants of "E-bo-la!" and "Syph-ill-is!!" as strains of bacteria competed to colonize my toothbrush. Somewhat ominously, there was a boulder-sized hole in the floor covered by a thin, dirty strip of carpet. The K. had all the allure of shabbily upholstered pus, but it did offer a quick way to get downstairs to breakfast.

We stayed in other bad hotels, but the most charmingly horrid one was in London. The hotel was named for St. S., an Eastern European ascetic who demonstrated his piety through self-mortification: for the 40 days of Lent, he neither ate nor drank. In later years he upped the guilt ante by doing the whole thing standing up. When he tired of the luxe life of a monk, he built an unshaded 50-foot pillar, climbed to the top, and stayed there for 36 years.

We went to London so Andy could speak at an academic conference; the Saint S. was conveniently located and reasonably priced.

The hotel was run by a family held together by unshakeable bonds of mutual resentment and simmering hatred, ruled over by a menacing patriarch we will call Tomislav, who created an ambiance much like an Eastern European version of *Wuthering Heights*.

Tomislav exuded a grizzly-esque geniality and the charm of a swaying cobra. At check-in, he explained that we would have to pay in advance for all four nights. Like Mowgli mesmerized by Kaa, the snake in the *Jungle Book*, all four of us nodded in unison.

Obviously, we agreed to pay in advance, once we learned that the policy was the unfortunate result of irresponsible Italians who, on visits to London, spent all their cash on clothing and food, so they had no money for their hotel bill.

"Wait," you might say. "He told you that Italians, *Italians*, would blow all their money on *British food*, and *British fashion*? And because of that, he demanded you pay in advance?"

"RUUUUN!!" you are shouting. "He's lying! Never pay a hotel up front!!"

Ah, such innocence. We were the babysitter in a slasher flick. Sure, we got that call asking us to check on the children who were sleeping in the cellar, and we were puzzled by the caller's jagged breath. *Say,* was that a bloody footprint on the mat when we came in? But we didn't run away, and what happened next was our own dang fault.

Andy turned over our credit card, and one swipe later, we were czeched into the Saint S. Hotel.

The kids and I used the stairs, while Andy was trapped with the owner in a frail elevator the size of Saint S.'s perch. Tomislav brought us to Room 14, or maybe he was showing us a postage stamp. The room's three beds and four towels all overlapped, and the sole armoire had the dimensions and heft of an upended tissue box. Eaves like obese stalactites jutted from the ceiling; at 6'4", Andy would knock himself unconscious turning over in bed. We were not convinced that Room 14 was going to work, so Tomislav graciously offered a larger room.

Room 18 had a ceiling, so things were already looking up. The bathroom was clean and neatly tiled, and we were too tired to notice the lack of soap. Or that if there had been soap, there wouldn't be enough room to close the door. But there was a huge window overlooking the rooftops of London, the beds looked comfortable, and this was London, where a hotel room costs as much as a room in a London hotel. Besides, we had already paid.

The next morning, we learned the many reasons the hotel was named for a martyr. The shower head didn't attach to the wall, so getting clean required juggling water and shampoo while trying to fend off the filmy shower curtain, which relentlessly clung to our eyelids while flinging every drop onto the bathroom floor.

Andy availed himself of the hotel's only amenity, an electrical outlet. When he plugged in his razor, it let out a puff of smoke, and to the kids' delight, the razor exploded. Fortunately, no one was hit by flying shrapnel, and Andy's half-grizzled, half-shaved face gave him the rakish appeal sought after by London academics.

The day had a rough start, but Tomislav had promised us a breakfast featuring the best of British and Serbian cuisine. When I got downstairs, Andy and the kids were already seated at a wooden table heaped with food. Well, it was not exactly food, but there were a million little plates with odd looking items smothered under Saran Wrap. My arrival triggered a new volley of plate delivery, although in a week, the four of us couldn't have eaten what was heaped in front of us.

A single dish held three kinds of bread that looked and tasted like several grades of sandpaper. Splayed under plastic were slices of fruit from which all color and texture had been drained. Other dishes entombed antique donuts, prehistoric rolls, and slivers of gummy cheese that tasted more like medical tubing than milk.

A pale young woman brought fluids reminiscent of coffee, tea, and hot chocolate, but they were diluted to tastelessness, and cold. I felt guilty for the food we tasted but could not eat, and for her carpal tunnel damage from all that wrapping.

On the way upstairs, I was grilled about breakfast and agreed with Tomislav that it was a bounteous repast. Andy attempted small talk, but the conversation quickly went north: "Who was your favorite American president in the last 50 years?" demanded Tomislav. "Besides Kennedy! Everyone says Kennedy!!"

Andy ventured, "Clinton."

"Clinton bombed my country," Tomislav noted darkly. When we mentioned we had seen the Diana and Dodi memorial at Harrod's, he muttered, "The Queen killed them both. It's printed in the British papers, so it must be true."

With no usable electricity or water, the Saint S. was a drain on our budget and our mood. His presentation over, and on the verge of his 50th birthday, Andy plotted our escape during our second plastic breakfast.

On his laptop, Andy found a mystical land just outside of London, where hotels had luxury items, like soap. Two rooms for two nights at a boring corporate hotel, with tickets to Legoland Windsor thrown in, cost less than one room at the Motel Martyr.

But we had already paid for all four nights.

Andy approached Tomislav warily. He asked for a refund for the two nights we wouldn't use, and Tomislav explained that their cancellation policy required 48 hours' notice. Andy pointed out that it was still 48 hours from the fourth day, so he could refund one night. "No! You stay for four nights! This is a good hotel, and you will stay with us."

The next morning Andy left to pick up a getaway car while I wrestled with the shower. The kids had granola bars, but by 11 a.m. I was desperate for caffeine. To get to the dining room I would have to pass the registration desk, but at 11:45 Andy hadn't returned. Should I tell them we were checking out, and risk having our bags and possibly ourselves dumped onto the sidewalk? It was August in London, so of course it was damp and cold. What if Andy didn't get back for hours?

In a desperate gambit for resuscitative caffeine, I bravely descended to the lobby to say we were leaving and asked what the hotel would prefer— should we remove our luggage so they could clean the room? "No," Tomislav Jr. replied. "You're here until Friday."

"Yes, but our plans have changed—my husband has rented a car and we're going to Windsor. We won't need the room."

"No, you don't need a car. Windsor is 20 minutes by train. You stay here and take the train to Legoland. You have already paid."

Trapped in Hotel Hell with no hope of rescue, I smiled demurely at the foolishness of my American husband.

"Could I have some tea?" I asked, as if a cup of tea would bring my husband to his senses; I knew it would work wonders for mine.

"Of course, would you like breakfast?"

"No, tea is fine."

On my way back upstairs, Tomislav stopped me. "Did you have breakfast?"

"No, thank you, tea is fine."

"Take it up on the lift!" he ordered. I walked onto the tiny elevator, and he stepped inside.

"Have breakfast!!" he demanded.

"No, really, tea is fine."

"Should I wake you for breakfast tomorrow morning?"

"No, thank you."

"Is there anything else I can get you?"

"No, really..."

Finally he stepped aside, the doors wheezed shut, and I sucked down the tea before the lift got to the second floor.

Andy got back around noon. When we brought down our luggage and asked for our money back, Tomislav's son demanded to know why we were leaving. Glaring at his father, he shouted, "Is there anything wrong?! Tell me anything that is wrong with this hotel, why you do not want to stay here!!"

Not wanting to star in an Iron Curtain episode of *Family Feud*, Andy demurred that we would like to stay, but our plans had changed.

"See!! I told you!!" shouted Tomislav. "This man speaks the truth!! He does not bullshit!! He does not say that this is broken, or that the hotel is dirty!! This man speaks the truth!!"

We escaped with one night refunded and a voucher for a free night at the Saint S. Because I like you, and I know you like breakfast, that is our gift to you.

Apparently, Simeon achieved sainthood for staying all four nights.

Chapter 46
Reality Bites

I have so far resisted talking about Italian food. Americans who go to Italy all write about the amazing cuisine. It's impossible to read about Italian food without getting viciously hungry. Unless you are in a restaurant in Italy, you cannot have what they're having, so to describe what it is like to *live* this food is cruel.

In an American pantry, it's hard to find freshly made, hand-stuffed pumpkin ravioli in fresh butter and basil. If you read about great food, you must satisfy yourself with what is readily available. Then you and a bag of Cheetos get sucked into a downward shame spiral from which you emerge with orange fingers and tight pants. I couldn't buy new pants; I know how important it is to maintain one's clothing size. So for your sake, I'm trying to keep you from making a beeline for the salty snack aisle. (All right, *go*, but at *least* buy a small bag.)

I loved the food in Italy, but I didn't feel like writing about it. Because 87 percent of my time in Modena was spent cooking, cleaning up, washing clothes with food on them, trudging to the store to buy groceries, and dodging traffic to carry it home. When you lived with a teenage boy who was growing exponentially and ate his weight at every meal, writing about food was like an inmate writing about cell door design: why wallow?

Writing about Italian food made me tired; eating it made me cry. The first time I had pizza there, tears ran onto the perfectly crisp crust. I'm a vegetarian, so vegetables rule. Pizza there offered toppings from all over the produce aisle: artichoke, eggplant, peppers, zucchini and onions, spinach. And a variety of cheeses: gorgonzola, parmigiana, different types of mozzarella (*fior di latte* is made from cow's milk, *fior di latte di bufala* from water buffalo milk), provolone. Pizza dough cooks very quickly, so if you use fresh vegetables, the toppings are crunchy and can be bitter. There the veggies are marinated in olive oil, gently roasted, then seared into melted cheese.

Pizza was a revelation, but there was so much else to eat, even for a vegetarian. When I first tried tortelloni in butter and basil, I understood why butter should be served fresh. Fresh melted butter is a handful of sunshine splashed across the plate. Ligurian *trofie* with plump green beans and pesto is comfort food made magnificent.

Just like home. NOT!!

My relationship with Italy was sadly dysfunctional, because of the food. When postal employees refused to sell me stamps because They. Must. Weigh. Each. Letter. Of. Each. Word. *before* I sealed the envelope, I was enraged. But all it took was a cup of cappuccino and I loved them again. A cloud of milk sprinkled with sugar and swirled into perfectly roasted coffee made every cup a short but memorable visit to heaven. Why be mad? When I couldn't buy a cellphone without providing seven forms of identification, just a single scoop of gelato and I forgave Italy everything. So help me, I was Hillary Clinton, and Italy was my Bill.

Italian produce, even the hack produce at the supermarket, was fresher than the crates of Styrofoam sold at Costco. Slice into an Italian carrot, and the blade is slick with juice. Garlic cloves bead with moisture when cut. Mushrooms are packed just as they're harvested: with balls of soil clinging to the rounded bottoms. The fruit is heavy and sweet. Blood oranges, iridescent with intense flavor, are an explosion of fireworks to satisfy all of your senses. Grapes have both a tang and the mellowness of good rain and steady sunshine.

Italian produce is sold locally, I probably ate grapes from vines I could see from the train, and it was sold in season, so in the grocery store, there were no Brussels sprouts in the spring, there was no broccoli until the fall. Growers don't use wax or preservatives, so vegetables spoiled quickly. Peppers lasted four days at most, green beans dried out and broccoli yellowed in three days. So you stopped at the market every day, cooked everything immediately, and savored every bite.

Even snack food there brushed greatness. *Classica* potato chips are thick, crunchy, not greasy. Cheese puffs aren't neon orange and metallic with chemicals; they shed flakes of real parmesan.

And the cheese—oh my, the cheese. American provolone tastes like a pencil eraser, but Italian provolone is nutty, mellow. Provolone *piccante* (sharp, not spicy) was a transformative experience. Fresh grated parmesan added shards of brilliance to anything it fell on. I took the stairs, so the cheese didn't transform my thighs into mozzarella.

I tried to cook Italian. No more bottled lemon juice. I bought a bag of fresh lemons and squeezed them over everything. It was easy: try Brussels sprouts roasted in the oven with olive oil, garlic, and the juice of one whole lemon. I remember the frozen, pale olive wads my mom boiled and plopped in a bowl; the citizens of Brussels should demand reparations for what Americans did to their good name.

In Italy, every dish awakens your senses. Salad starts with fresh greens with all of the aroma of newly cut grass. I added sliced carrot, fresh tomatoes, olive oil. And balsamic vinegar, which is made in Modena in a loving, patient process that takes a minimum of 12 to 25 years. American balsamic vinegar is painfully acidic, but aging makes balsamic sweet. A great bottle of old Modena *aceto* costs 180 euros, and you can eat it with a spoon. But after only 12 summers in a wooden cask, traditional *aceto* pools on the lettuce and flirts with the olive oil; every bite tells you why those two have stayed together all these years.

I have no idea what the odd implements in our kitchen drawer were used for. But in an act of pure kindness, Giovanna taught me to make risotto from scratch. It's not as hard as I thought: you sauté rice in olive oil, add broth (I saved the broth from broccoli for that), wine, Parmigiano Reggiano, a pinch of saffron, and you made a pot of molten gold. It was easy to make lasagna when the local supermarket sold sheets of soft pasta. You layer it with balls of mozzarella (getting those out of the bag always made me laugh), sauce, vegetables, and more cheese. I made another pan and layered the vegetables with pesto. And I loved to roast new potatoes with slivers of fresh onion, drizzled with olive oil, and sprinkled with a sprig of fragrant rosemary..

You could buy tiny jars of pasta sauce, but they were expensive. So I bought a bottle of tomato puree and made my own. The spices were more intense there; the first time I used Italian black pepper, the same amount I'd use at home, the sauce growled. The best tomato sauce? I used to load it up with basil, oregano, and garlic. But Andy made the best marinara I've ever had, and it was so simple: he sautéed onions and mushrooms in butter, added pureed tomato, and simmered. To make it taste authentic, you didn't even need to add spices, and now I don't like the heaviness of more complicated sauce.

Soup was satisfying: roasted vegetables, cabbage sautéed in butter with vegetable stock, and some beans. Mmmmn. Or creamy potato soup with fresh grated parmesan and cheese toast.

We never had leftovers, so my favorite lunch was fresh *pugliese* bread, provolone *piccante*, salad greens, tomatoes, and sweet balsamic vinegar. With *Classica* chips. It was best eaten overlooking the rooftops of Modena. And I miss our Friday night supper: takeout from *Pizzeria Ragno*, around the corner. For months I was hooked on *Verdure*: eggplant, onions, and zucchini, but then I discovered *Arcadia*: eggplant, mozzarella, provolone, and *parmigiana*. So many flavors, all found in nature.

Told ya so. You shouldn't have read this, because now you're hungry. I'm hungry, and I'm missing mussels sautéed in garlic and butter with the juice of two lemons, artichoke ravioli, mushroom tortellini, sliced fruit, and hearty *pugliese* bread for the broth.

Most nights, I went into the tiny, blue-tiled kitchen, took up a sharp knife, and sliced and sautéed and stirred, while listening to Pavarotti. I chopped and stirred and sautéed until my arm stopped working, and only then had I made enough to tide Alex over until dessert. Only if Andy were there to help cook, was it physically possible to make too much for Alex to consume. I chopped, and I stirred, and Pavarotti and I looked out my little window onto the roofs of Modena, and I didn't feel like writing about food, I was too busy living it.

Chapter 47
Birthday List

Every year on my birthday, I make a bucket list in reverse—a list of the things I did for the very first time. What did I do, for the first time, that year?

Here's my list for our year in Italy:

1. Quit my job at a staff meeting. Still smiling about that.

2. Figured out what to pack to live for a year in Italy. Still don't know.

3. Bought a cellphone, a bus pass, a train ticket, groceries, and contact lenses in Italian. It's not so scary, after you've done it 700 times.

4. Grew tomatoes on my balcony.

5. Made risotto, from scratch.

6. Bought pants at the open-air market, then bought some that fit, and even returned the ones that didn't. Lots of learning, there.

7. Climbed to the top of the Eiffel Tower, took a boat ride on the Seine, strolled along the Champs-Élysées, and climbed the Arc de Triomphe. All on the same day.

8. Took an overnight train to Paris, and another from Gdansk to Katowice, Poland, and one from Amsterdam to Denmark. Like sleeping in a blender, except there's no sleeping.

9. Had Welsh rarebit in Wales, an English muffin in England, and pierogies in Poland.

10. Talked to a Palestinian about living in Israel, a Bulgarian about living in China, and my mom's cousin about living with my great-grandmother. So many stories.

11. Went snorkeling on the Cote d'Azur, where we stayed in a lovely villa with my fascinating cousins.

12. Seared by Anne Frank's house, Oscar Schindler's factory, and the remains of the Jewish ghetto in Krakow.

13. Met Andy's Polish relatives. For the first time in my life, I loved people I could communicate with only by hugs and smiles.

14. Using only my crack navigational skills, took my kids on the Tube in London, the metro in Brussels, and a water taxi in Amsterdam. And found the hotel every time. Phew.

15. Went to Legoland Denmark, Legoland Windsor, and MiniEurope in Brussels. The fried fish in Legoland Denmark tastes like bilge spew. In MiniEurope, which had menus printed in English, French, and Belgian, ate in a restaurant that looked unnervingly like a cheesy Mexican place in the US. They served mayo with the burrito, a first, which was disconcerting in any language.

16. Saw the Gdansk shipyard where Lech Walesa started a movement that brought down the Iron Curtain. Amazing stuff can happen in ordinary parking lots.

17. Got a scary spider bite, which bloomed into a raised ring o' pain. Ew.

18. Saw Ferraris and Maseratis in their native habitat, on the streets of Italy. The paint, like the engine, simmmmmers.

19. Rode my bike to the grocery store. And lived.

20. Bought a beaded gown in an Italian shop, with Italian ladies cooing over the dress. Priceless.

21. Flew to the Canary Islands. Didn't see any canaries.

22. Fell in love with Van Gogh's electric brush strokes, and Pavarotti's soaring voice: he sings in the colors of Modena.

23. Walked Omaha Beach in Normandy. Understood the bravery of American and British soldiers who landed in the surf and had to cross a beach and climb cliffs while under fire from German machine gunners. Those soldiers, boys really, broke the back of evil, and we can't forget their sacrifice.

24. Started a blog.

25. Spent ten hours in the Louvre, six hours in Westminster Abbey, and hundreds of hours in a million museums learning with my kids. My kids are awesome.

26. Floated in the aquamarine glass of the Ligurrrian Sea. One of my favorite things, ever.

27. Picked up beach glass in Sardegna. Sardegnians must spend most of their time hurling windows and bottles into the sea, or they wouldn't have so much beach glass.

28. Had gelato shaped like a flower petal and learned how to say my favorite flavors: *amarena,* (cherry) *malaga, fior di latte.*

29. Talked to a plumber about water pressure in Italian.

30. Went to an *acetaia*, an Italian farmhouse where they make traditional balsamic vinegar. On the way home, watched my mom's cousin and her husband scramble into—and out of—a drainage ditch as we all ran to catch the bus back to Modena. They were in their 70s. That wasn't the first time we regretted not having a car in Italy, but it was probably the best reason to regret not having a car in Italy. If you're going to invite relatives to Italy, make sure they're as amazing as Clare and Eric.

31. On the 1 a.m. train back from Venice, my brain had to simultaneously process: (1) the guy in the seat behind us wearing full "Joker" makeup: white face, red lips, black jagged lines radiating from his mouth and eyes; (2) Alex sneezing uncontrollably; (3) a Sikh in a bright orange turban asking politely whether this was the train to Parma. Italy at 1 a.m. is complicated.

32. Tried grappa. Grappa tastes like what you'd drink with the fried fish at Legoland Denmark.

33. Rode in a gondola on the Grand Canal.

34. Ate at a Pompeii restaurant that serves authentic ancient Roman food. The precursor to lasagna was good, but the sauce—heavy on the oil and the anchovies—tasted an awful lot like the bad fish at Legoland Denmark. On the train back to Naples, feared Alex would be offed by a seething Naples thug. Terrifying.

35. Saw the Coliseum. And the Roman Forum. And the Pantheon. And the Sistine Chapel, and St. Peter's. And threw a coin in Trevi Fountain, three times. Every day, I learned how little I know about Italian history.

36. Bought Italian-made boots, finished outside and inside. On the outside, glossy black leather. On the inside, buttery suede at the foot, soft beige leather above the ankle. Exquisite. *Grazie*, Luca Christian Cotti, aka *Il Prof*.

37. Saw London from the London Eye.

38. Rode on a boat down the Thames.

39. Saw Shakespeare's school, and his grave.

40. Saw Stonehenge.

41. Did our laundry in Bath.

42. Tried to syndicate blog stories several times. Was rejected several times.

43. Responded to a rejection letter with the closing line, "Perhaps you can spend *next* Friday evening clubbing baby seals."

44. Celebrated the end of Easter Mass in Notre Dame Cathedral. Although the church is ponderously dark, during Mass, music and candles soften the massive

stones. The service ended with a surge of the organ, rolling waves of sound that brushed the Rose Windows and brought heaven close enough to hear.

45. Watched Murano glassblowers turn molten blobs into a crystal horse and a vase.

46. Saw the statue of David, three times. Still smiling.

47. Climbed the 666 portici to Bologna's San Luca.

48. Saw the Giro d'Italia. Didn't actually see it, the bikes went by so fast.

49. Saw Mont-Saint Michel, a church in France that is built on an island that is cut off from the land with the tide.

50. Ate *lody*—Polish ice cream—an eight-inch tower of swirled chocolate or vanilla. It's almost all butterfat, so it doesn't melt, like eating a stick of butter.

51. Walked in the Race for the Cure, Bologna.

52. Went to an Italian soccer match.

53. Watched my kids eat blackberries in Wales. Watched my son return some, in the back of the rental car. Ew.

54. Saw Dante's house, and the church where he was married.

55. Saw Galileo's grave, and Machiavelli's.

56. Had dinner by myself in Vernazza, one of the little towns of Cinque Terre. Watched cops arrest a drunken guitarist.

57. Read my favorite short story—written by Edith Wharton, it's about two women, romantic rivals, who visit Rome—in Italian. Reading it in another language made me slow down and savor the words.

58. Watched my son cook his own pasta sauce, my daughter order in Italian, and my kids laugh about the differences between British and American English. We've all learned so much.

59. Climbed a million bell tower steps and was in one when the bells went off. Every cell vibrated with the amazing sound.

Now your turn: every year, on your birthday, make a list of the things you did for the first time this year. Make it better than this one.

Chapter 48
Modena Remembers 9-11

Modena is my heart's home. My attempts to navigate its streets and culture made me laugh, its infinite beauty made me cry. I was *una straniera*, but one morning in September, I felt the city's warm embrace. This lovely town holds a piece of America: a statue that commemorated America's losses on 9-11.

As I shrank from the sting of yet another icy shower, I heard voices. Not the usual ones, telling me to call my landlord to complain about the lack of hot water, but deep Italian ones, from outside. I peered over the balcony and saw that a crowd had gathered in the piazza in front of our apartment building.

The piazza is ringed by a chaotic traffic circle, but in the center of the circle is a grassy area with an odd bit of sculpture: two chunks of metal enclosed in circular bands of steel. I assumed it was an Italian war monument, until I read the plaque: It's a memorial to 9-11.

Modena is a city of delightful surprises; it was Pavarotti's birthplace, and it holds one of the most sought-after restaurants in the world. But Modena also holds a piece of New York; two sections of steel girders from the World Trade Center, enclosed in open steel spheres, stand on twin concrete towers, an Italian tribute to 9-11.

The memorial was the first thing we saw when we got off the bus from the airport. I'd never seen anything like that outside of New York, yet this small town not only put up a memorial, but on the eighth anniversary of 9-11, they held a service, in remembrance.

The crowd was gathered around the monument. I threw on shorts and a shirt, tried to smooth my wet hair, and slipped to the back of the crowd.

The piazza bristled with uniforms. There were generals, policemen, and dignitaries in elegant Italian suits. But other people were casually dressed in jeans and sandals. More than 50 Italians attended the ceremony. They all came to stand with America and remember its tragedy. I felt my wild hair curl and unfurl in the light breeze.

The memorial was flanked by flags—tall stately banners representing the City of Modena, Lion's Club International, and *Leo*, the Italian Lion's Club. The statue's rusted girders were softened by rich cloth in jewel tones; the flags held proudly aloft by caring people half a world and eight years from the day the Towers fell. There were two huge laurel wreaths, regal with gold ornaments and gilded velvet ribbons. Off to the right, a fire engine waited.

Several dignitaries spoke, of the fallen, of our unity, and of a global need for peace. I heard the words *Stati Uniti* and was deeply honored: this town has suffered Nazis, Fascists, and the bubonic plague, and yet these people chose to share America's sorrow. And America doesn't even know they are here.

At the close of the speeches, the fire engine siren wailed briefly like the wild grief of a bagpipe. Standing at attention next to the truck were the *vigili del fuoco*, firefighters. They are the Italian brothers of the heroes of 9-11, and these are the people who walk into hell for us.

I always wondered who built the monument, and that day I met the man who spent three years ensuring that Modena would remember. His name is Paolo, and he looks like a New York skyscraper: he's tall and steely in a gray suit with steady gray eyes. He's from Modena but had moved to New York and was in the city when the towers fell. Paolo walked to Ground Zero and stared at the jagged shards of the building that stood long after the rest had gone to earth. His eyes lowered with the memory. Paolo said the city smelled like smoke and burning plastic for three months.

Paolo asked whether he could take some pieces of the World Trade Center to Italy. Working with the Lion's Club, the *Leo* Club, and the City of Modena, Paolo and his friends raised money for the project. It took three years to bring the girders here, build the statue, and dedicate the monument.

Paolo now lives in New York. Looking at the monument, Paolo said it was hard not to cry, because he remembers.

Paolo applied for US citizenship and would be an American citizen within the year.

Welcome to America, Paolo, and thank you. Thank you, Lion's Club. *Grazie, Leo* Club, *Grazie* Modena.

We will remember you, too.

Chapter 49
If These Walls Could Talk

In Europe, I read the walls. Historians stack facts, organize events, and bind them into books, but the history of ordinary people is hanging on plaques all over Europe. As I walked in Italy, I searched the walls for the marble manuscripts that haunt public spaces.

Plaques—in iron, in marble, in stone—marked the homes of politicians, poets, and painters, but also the places where lives were lost, so every generation will forever remember the people who lived and died for Italy. But the people who died were also the people who once read the walls. These walls not only stand for remembrance, they span history, and unite generations.

Strolling through the small Italian town of Ferrara, history murmured from every facade. Watching over a street that has bordered a neighborhood since the Renaissance, a simple villa of grayed stone held an elaborate marble plaque nestled next to a small square window that embraced the entrails of a long-dead potted plant. According to the plaque, the poet who lived here quite literally captured the imagination of Italy. I didn't write down his name, and an internet search told me only that in 1602, Ferrara bustled with wandering poets. Imagine a town of poets, wondering at walls.

Imagine.

On another street, another tribute hung in silent sunlight:

A devoto ricordo
di tutti coloro che sotto
questa mura cercando
refugio persero la vita
per bombardiemento aero.
28 gennaio 1944

Here is the translation:

"Devoted to the memory
of those who under this wall
lost their lives seeking refuge
from aerial bombardment"
January 28, 1944"

Oh.

People died, *here.* They crouched against *this* wall while bombs fell. Ten years later, in 1954, their grieving families etched those lives into history.

A third plaque hangs on the wall of the Ferrara train station. This one buckled my knees.

"Oh, $(#*!" I blurted, and my son was shocked, but this is what it says:

In questa stazione
il 19 Ottobre 1943
Sosto il treno della Shoah
con 1023 Ebrei di Roma
Diportate dei Nazi
verso lo stermino di Auschwitz

"In this station, on October 19, 1943, the Shoah Train stopped, carrying 1,023 Roman Jews who were deported by the Nazis and taken to extermination in Auschwitz."

No.

These walls have shadowed poets, strolling lovers, lagging children. Sometimes they offered refuge, from sun, from rain, from bombs. The Ferrara train station has always been crowded with families. But Ferrarans left a stone-cold reminder that other families—Jewish parents, children, aunts, uncles, cousins, and grandparents—fought for breath in a cattle car, rolling toward death, right here.

If these walls could talk? They do. You just have to know what they say.

Chapter 50
Italy Is God's Attic

My Modena is a painting, with a million strokes, of shade and light and subtle color. It's a thousand years of history; the cobblestoned Via Emilia was built by the Romans and runs to the sea. The streets resound with bells that for centuries have marked the hours and warned the town of approaching danger. My artist friend Piero told me that there is a language of bells; when he was a boy, every morning at 6 a.m., bells rang out the day's weather: one bell for sun, two for clouds, three for rain, and four for snow. In the evening, while people pass below, the bells call to each other: "Are you still there?"

"For eternity, like you."

"Till we meet again, my friends."

Without a car, I walked in Modena to live, but I also lived to walk. I had favorite rambles that satisfied every one of my senses. My walks began in Piazza Grande, an ancient square studded with rounded cobbles gracefully traversed by Italian women in stilettos.

Perched on the edge of the piazza is the Duomo, a grand dame draped in a luxurious stone cloak in vari-colored blocks of rose and creamy marble, like the coat from Gustav Klimt's "The Kiss." Behind her is the bell tower, the Torre della Ghirlandina, which for years was sheathed in restoration scaffolding, but has emerged like a butterfly from her chrysalis.

In one of my final weeks in Modena, I had a few hours to myself, so I struck out for my usual haunts. As I passed the Duomo, and its two medieval lions standing guard before the battered wooden door, I heard the organ playing. The door was locked, so I stood outside and listened. I love the power of church organs, but not the sound. Church organ music can be an annoying blither of ecclesiastical kvetching, or a towering crunch of cacophony, a loud and loutish smudge.

But not this time. This organist literally pulled out all the stops. He tore up and down the scale in soaring crescendos, crystalline arpeggios, the music so monumental it could flutter the wings of angels. Outside the church, I gloried in the melodic surge, a thousand tones swaying in harmony from every stone surface, falling lightly to my ears in the square. Heaven sounds just like that.

Inside the Duomo - Pavarotti Sang in The Choir Here

The organ fell quiet, so I moved on to the front of the Duomo, with its carved beasts of every description, and its two lions, snarling in agony with their stone faces upturned. To the right of the Duomo, there is a secret street, Via San Eufemia, where buildings gently embrace, shutting out the cars and noise, where old Italy lies.

Italy is God's attic. Nestled between utilitarian spaces where people live, shop, and work, churches provide strength and comfort. Italian families gather there for worship, for baptisms and burials. For a jaded American accustomed to big box stores of stultifying sameness and graceless chapel beams of raw oak, Italian churches are gloriously disconcerting.

When I first arrived, I was afraid to open doors. I was afraid to step inside, because I wouldn't know what to say when I got there. But now, in the freedom of language and leaving, I tried every door. Italy has 1,600 churches; tiny Venice has over 100 of them. Modena has so many this town feels like a living Advent Calendar. And every time I pushed open a church door, I was astonished at their age, and art, and architecture.

One of my favorites is La Chiesa di San Barnaba. You would never know from her facade, but inside, she is as tiny and as gilded as a Faberge egg. I walked into San Barnaba for the first time one evening in the middle of a service—and the church was so small that when I entered, *I* was in the middle of the service. The mass, in Italian, held the velvet hush of bowed heads and softly rolling vowels.

Still in awe over San Barnaba's trompe l'oeil ceilings that were painted to look like carved marble, I meandered down a cobblestone street, peering up at shutters hung centuries ago. Above the street, on the corner of a building, is perched a terracotta bust of the aristocrat who once owned this palazzo, a Modenese gentleman in sienna clay who has greeted visitors for 500 years.

The street ended in a long block of gray stone, with light radiating from a doorway cut into a dingy wall. I pushed on the glass doors. They didn't open, but a workman in gray overalls stepped up to help me: the doors slide apart. I stepped inside, and there was *La Chiesa di Sant Agostino*, a mammoth Renaissance behemoth built on a majestic scale. Columns as thick as sequoias were topped with massive marble angels, pilasters, carving of every description. The ceiling was a series of murals—Moses with the stone tablets, the Ark. The marble and the paintings were dimmed by the smoke of centuries, but the audacity of the spectacle was impressive. And the altar, a wall of carved gold, glowed.

All this, through a doorway I'd passed by a hundred times. My mouth would not close—how does Modena have so many treasures? And fabulous shoes, too??? There are churches like this all over Italy, and each time I entered one, I was overwhelmed by a feeling of hushed serenity, of the greatness of a God that can coax such beauty from believers. And by the thought of so much money spent by the wealthy to secure a spot in heaven.

San D'Agostino was amazing. But I had more time, and more places to see. There was a bicycle shop, "Bicycles Equipment, and Books or Curiosity," which looked like a shop window from *It's a Wonderful Life*. The window display held artfully arranged antique bicycles, books, and old valises. How did Italians *do* this? Make ordinary objects look like movie sets, make a walk so enchanting?

I had never been to the Duomo Museum, so I stopped in. I was alone;

lights clicked on as I entered each room. Filled with the treasures of the
Duomo, the small museum proudly displayed golden candlesticks, chalices,
and reliquaries, elaborate containers for sacred relics. And there were vest-
ments, creamy silk embroidered with the palette of spring: powder blues,
blush pinks, the fresh green of new shoots.

On the staircase of the Duomo Museum, the sound of a voice lesson
warmed the chill air. A soprano was practicing *"Adeste Fideles."* She sang in
Italian, and her voice was more beautiful because she couldn't quite control it.
When a note went wrong, it sounded of burnished suede, but when she found
the pitch, it was the lightest silk, floating to the sky. All of this in a museum
stairwell; I was grateful there was no elevator.

Walking back on Via Emilia, a road built by Romans, I strolled beneath
portici that sheltered fascinating shops; I savored every window. My favorite was a
lingerie store. Such confections in lace and satin, on mannequins that revolved to
show off every curve. A black satin thong was topped with a jeweled clasp. Not a
place I would put glitter, but Italian bodies are made for that kind of thing.

I walked home, having had my fill of all my senses. In two hours, I'd scaled
the clouds on notes from bells, an organ, and a soprano. My eyes shimmered
from the Duomo soaked in sunlight, the glittering letters of the bicycle shop,
the spires of the ecclesiastical candlesticks. I'd felt the cool air on my skin, and
tasted the satisfaction of having lived well.

This was my Modena, and this I would miss. But for now, I had to wash
some clothes, and maybe Fabio was on the balcony…

Chapter 51
Epilogue

Every morning of 2009, I awoke to the walls of my Italian bedroom. I'd see and smell paint applied just after the founding of Rome, and smile: "We're still in Italy!!" Not today. This morning I woke in my own room, in Colorado. I love my bedroom—it's airy and light, with periwinkle walls and silky cream sheets. The paint in my Modena apartment wasn't as much a hue as it was a residue of passing years, brushed with mold, and laced with cobwebs. Beyond the windows, the sienna scales of ruffled rooftops skittered above streets that wandered like poets lost in thought. The colors of Modena, the shades of history and endless expectation, were back in that apartment. And next week, the apartment would have fresh paint, for Giovanna's daughter's lovely family.

If I had stayed until the walls were redone, getting me on the plane would have required sedation. If our apartment had any water pressure, a washing machine that didn't require a full-time assistant to keep it running, or maybe just an occasional splash of hot water for bathing and washing dishes, I would have wanted to stay forever.

Because what I left behind in Modena was an inherently interesting life. Every Monday in Modena, at the open-air market, where the bazaar meets the bizarre, I might find the perfect purple sweater, or a great jacket for 15 euros, but just riffling through heaps of fabric was endlessly entertaining. Modena also held Elena's skeptical laugh, Piero's sun-softened studio, Annamaria's homemade pasta, Giovanna's smile, and the beauty of Michele and Yael, a gorgeous young couple who would make Italy what it would be next. And bells and buildings and fabulous art.

Living in Italy was heaven for me, like a perpetual afternoon in the library of a long-abandoned palace, with hours to explore shelves of intimate treasures: illuminated manuscripts, illustrated histories, carefully folded love letters and momento-stuffed diaries. In Modena, a city made modern by people who pre-dated the Romans, every building was a volume of secrets, every view held exquisite surprises, of rich color and the living work of long-dead artists.

Heaven for me is an endless museum. But although I lived in my idea of paradise, I had to function in most Americans' idea of hell. Italy is not efficient. Italy is not convenient. Living in Italy is not particularly comfortable. It's a fabulous place to relax, but it's a challenge to accomplish anything more ambitious than lunch.

The most basic tasks were insanely complex. How do you ship a box to the United States? The shipping rules of the Italian post office depended on the day, on the post office, on the mood of a particular employee, maybe the pollen count. The rules were never the same once, never mind during multiple transactions. Trying to complete a simple task in Italy was like trying to fill out a mortgage application while being tossed about by drunken pirates. Every transaction was a swashbuckling adventure into what I didn't know.

But what marvelous things there were to learn! Where does this conga line of ochre buildings lead, whose heroism does this plaque remember, how does every fruit stand look like it was created by a Renaissance painter? What made each generation of Italians preserve all this, so that terracotta trim and the roar of a marble lion still catch the afternoon sun after 500, 800, 1,000 years?

Italians have always made an art of living, and they still do. Italians today transform automotive steel into raw power and growling desire. Italians create edible art, spend hours enjoying it, and orchestrate every outfit like they're staging a private opera. Italy doesn't hide its beauty in museums, or within the pages of magazines. Italian beauty is woven into everyday life, so the packets of sugar on the counter of a coffee bar are a fanned and festive sculpture, and the display of even ordinary objects (nail clippers! sewing kits!) beguiles the passerby.

Italians created a cult out of culture.

Such a fine basis for a civilization. If Italians decided to organize government as well as it organizes crime, establish a power grid that can support a microwave oven, and ask dog owners to pick up the poop under the *portici*, Italy would be the global winner in the "You Should Be Like Us" sweepstakes.

Back home, at my comfortable computer desk, with a tray that rolls out and carpeting beneath my feet, I can only remember the colors and sounds. I have so many memories, so many photographs. In the past year, we visited 50

European cities, many of them several times. We went to Rome in early spring, in blazing summer, and in dampening fall. The statue of David is an old friend. On the second visit, I spent 20 minutes just taking in the perfection of his calves. Great art takes time. Only on the third visit to the Sistine Chapel could I drop my eyes to the Botticellis surrounding the walls of the chapel, find all the places where Moses was painted, in green and yellow robes, and recognize a view of the Arch of Constantine in the Roman Forum. So many emperors, so much time. How do I learn enough to appreciate what I have seen?

That year we walked the beaches of Normandy, had dinner with Andy's relatives in Poland, and with mine in London. We skipped rocks in Sardegna, ate lasagna as it was served in ancient Pompeii, and retraced Galileo's steps up the tower in Pisa. We saw Dante's home in Florence, the church where he was married, and his tomb. On one of our last days in Italy, Piero gave us a watercolor he had painted of the Duomo, and Annamaria poured into my palm 300-year-old aceto, her family history distilled into thick, sweet drops. I not only lived in a museum; I ate in one.

Now that I'm home, I notice the differences. Everything in America is bigger. The streets, the cars, even the spaces between things, are all built on a larger scale. Toothbrushes look painfully swollen here, and mammoth stores sell them in sets of eight encased in packaging that can be opened only with wire cutters. How much plastic do we need to remove bacteria from our teeth? In Italy I bought juice glasses like some I had at home, but the American ones are double the size. Bigger glasses create bigger portions, even when you're just drinking water, which matters when you have to carry every drop three blocks. No wonder Americans have grown larger—our big cars carry big boxes over wide and unwalkable streets. Our bodies can't burn off enough calories to keep up with all of our effortless consumption.

In America, I am comfortable. Stores are always open; I can buy a lifetime supply of toothpaste at 3 a.m., I know how to mail a package, I can wash and dry a week's worth of clothes in a few hours and have time left over to read Dante. But I can't walk where Dante walked, I can't climb Galileo's tilted tower. I'm not spending an afternoon in an enchanted museum; I'm trapped in a 24/7 superstore. One that will sell me a million of anything I want, but that doesn't hold anything I need.

Modena changed me, but maybe it just showed me who I am.

Grazie, Giovanna. *Grazie*, Raimondo. *Grazie*, Piero. *Grazie*, Annamaria. *Grazie*, Elena. *Grazie*, Paolo. *Grazie,* Melanie.

Grazie, Modena.

Till we meet again, my friends.

ABOUT THE AUTHOR

Andrea Susan Valentine Gelfuso Goetz is an environmental attorney who adores Italy and all things Italian. A year in Italy with her husband and two kids, while living in an apartment that was like camping, with tile, and in a city that was like God's attic, made her appreciate Italian culture, art, and heart-stoppingly gorgeous Italians. Her book, My Modena, a Year of Fear, Laughter, and Exhilaration in Italy details the delightful confusion of living in a town that made every task hilariously frustrating, but every walk a journey into Italy's fascinating past - and thrilling present. *My Modena* is her first book.

Printed in Great Britain
by Amazon

66908664R00116